110-Day Devotional

to

PORTRAITS
OF
CHRIST

HUGH ANDERSON, II

Design and editing: Crystal J. Anderson

ISBN-10: 0692400648
ISBN-13: 978-0692400647

For Worldwide Distribution

Printed in the United States of America

To Fern.

CONTENTS

PREFACE

The inspiration for writing *Portraits of Christ: A Book of Sermons* and the accompanying sequel, *110-Day Devotional to Portraits of Christ*, was to reintroduce Jesus Christ to myself and to the world. I felt as though there was too much emphasis being placed on the negative things that were happening in the world socially, politically, economically, and a redefining of God and His Word, the Holy Bible. These discussions gave far too much publicity to Satan and his negative influences in the world. It is as though he was being pushed, lifted up, and glorified more than Jesus. A year and a half ago, the Spirit of the Lord compelled me to write and "lift up the name of Jesus." It was like the Holy Spirit engulfed my being, and with this revelation, I started to write and promote the name of Jesus. My mind was set on putting the emphasis back on Jesus Christ and pushing Him and the Word of God. Jesus said that 'If I be lifted up to the world, I will draw all men unto me.' Jesus gets the attention!

In these books, I just want to present Jesus as the Savior of the world, the great Restorer, the great Peace Maker, and the all encompassing Love for mankind—all of which are necessary 'in times like these.'

John 3:16

For God so loved the world that He gave His only begotten Son, that whosoever believes in Him shall not perish, but have everlasting life.

Jesus is the Great Deliverer in times of severe stress,
pain, hurt, disappointment, and dismay. People commit
suicide—even pastors—when Jesus clearly offers peace
and tranquility to everyone. We should allow Jesus to take
His rightful place in our hearts and minds, in our churches,
and in the world.

I see Jesus Christ as the answer for the problems of
man and the problem of evil in this world. Job experienced
it when he lost everything and faced death. I sense so
much hurt in the world, even when people try to hide it
behind the veils of their outward smiles. In the church as
well, people are afraid to open up about what they are
facing and what they are going through. We don't have to
go it alone! Jesus is our salvation and complete
deliverance!

With that, this is not just another project for fame or
fortune, but an offering of "the heart of a pastor" sharing
what a real commitment to Jesus will do in a person's life.
Jesus is the reason for our existence. Jesus is the one who
will grant unto us an abundant life. I just want to push
Jesus as the Supreme answer for us all for living a beautiful
life and enjoying that life in the beauty of holiness.

Prayerfully, it is my hope that we will all become
portraits of Christ—Christ's workmanship—growing
closer to what God wants us to be, as persons made in His
image and likeness.

Specifically, *The 110-Day Devotional to Portraits of Christ* is a compilation of devotionals and sermons. They stem from the thoughts and ideas of the primary book, *Portraits of Christ*, and flow into practical application, particularly with inclusion of the "Followers of Christ" section. It is intended to be a companion to the original book in terms of further emphasizing the characteristics, mission, life and personality of Jesus Christ. However, in this devotional, the emphasis is on "The Followers of Christ" or "The Workmanship of Christ" as the image and likeness of Jesus Christ. Therefore, instead of looking at Christ's word portrait only, we now look at applying the messages from the life of Christ into the life of the believer.

The *Portraits of Christ* pictured Jesus as Deity; the majestic Lord and King; the supreme deliverer and restorer; the immutable Lord; the Jesus of history and the Christ of faith—the God-Man; the great high priest; the servant of God, as the fulfillment of Old Testament prophecy; and the Revelation self-portrait of Himself as the King of Kings, the Lord of Lords, and the head of the church.

Now, the emphasis shifts to God's human creation. Therefore, each devotional and message presents points where the believer is encouraged to learn more about Jesus Christ and apply these lessons to their lives. This devotional is divided into three major sections:

1. Discipleship Series with four sermons (Each sermon has a discipleship component)

1. Someone's Watching You: Imitators, Mimickers, and Apery
2. It's in the Name of Jesus: Some Spiritual Qualities Found in the Name of Jesus
3. The Followers of Christ
4. The Marks of a Personal Relationship with God

II. The Workmanship of Christ section, which consists of 75 daily devotions, and

III. The Followers of Christ section, which consists of 35 daily devotions

What is contained in this devotional is for the purpose of winning and cultivating men and women into the Body of Christ. It is a beautiful portrait when Jesus can be seen in the lives of His followers—His workmanship. May the Lord God help us daily to grow in grace and cultivate qualities to become more like Him.

Rev. Hugh Anderson, II

DISCIPLESHIP SERIES

SERMON 1 |
SOMEONE'S WATCHING YOU:
IMITATORS, MIMICKERS, AND APERY

1 Corinthians 11:1
"Imitate me, just as I also imitate Christ." (NKJV)

1 Corinthians 4:16
"Therefore I urge you, imitate me." (NKJV)

1 Thessalonians 1:6
"And you became followers of us and the Lord, having received the word in much affliction, with joy of Holy Spirit." (NKJV)

1 Thessalonians 2:14
"For you, brethren, became imitators of the churches of God which are in Judea in Christ Jesus. For you also suffered the same things from your own countrymen, just as they did from the Judeans." (NKJV)

1 Thessalonians 3:7-9
"Therefore, brethren, in all our affliction and distress we were comforted concerning you by your faith. 8 For now we live, if you stand fast in the Lord. 9 For what thanks can we render to God for you, for all the joy with which we rejoice for your sakes before our God." (NKJV)

Philippians 3:17
"Brethren, join in following my example, and note those who so walk, as you have us for a pattern." (NKJV)

To "imitate" is to follow, as a model or an example—like an author's style or like an older brother.

14

To "mimic" is to copy an action, speech, or move often playfully or derisively, in an unthinking manner, or to impersonate, as a student acting out a teacher's moves behind his or her back (in a negative or derisive manner). "Apery" is when someone copies the words or behavior of another—a copycat. Apery is usually a silly imitation of another, to make fun of another person. This may be a comedian who gets paid for "laughs."

Being an imitator, mimic, or performing apery can be positive or negative, good or bad. Each of these forms of imitation can be beneficial or not. What we see from these definitions is that imitating someone is not always for the right reasons. Imitating someone in order to cause embarrassment or poking fun at someone simply to build themselves up is negative imitation. For example, there are people who want to lead a life of crime by looking at those who are involved in crime. Some people want to be like someone else simply because they admire their lifestyle, whether good or bad. Some people want to follow a career path because they see someone else doing it—not because they have the skills or abilities. There are people who want to pursue certain ministries because they see someone else doing it successfully—but they may not be called for that ministry. But, everyone has a purpose in life—and in the service of the Lord. There are people who simply are not happy with themselves and desire to be like someone else and not themselves. People must be encouraged to follow what suits them and not someone else. A person's abilities, skills, and (discovering one's) purpose in life must be the foundation for that choice. The positive side of imitating someone is that of learning how to perform a task, learning from a positive behavior of another, learning to benefit from the experiences of another, or to be encouraged to move forward into a specific area of life—or simply viewing someone as a positive role model. The fact is that someone is watching each of us and are gathering positive (or negative) vibes, or are simply learning from them. By so doing, the person is also benefitting and growing.

The bottom line is that as "followers" of Jesus Christ, we must be willing to be good examples of who we say we are wherever we go. What we do for Christ in His church and in His kingdom must first begin with a committed life of service to Jesus Christ. A person must first seek forgiveness for sins and become a disciple of the Lord—a true witness for Him. Remember, someone is watching you whether you know it or not. Do people look at you and desire to be like you? Do people look at you and benefit from what you have to offer? Do people admire your personality? Our children are watching us and are learning behaviors and habits from us. Do you care about how people see you? Do you care about contributing anything at all to society? What about your legacy? Do you care about leaving something that will be of value to your family, your community, and to your memory? These are critical questions for many, and others simply do not care.

Followers of Christ should be concerned about how people view us because Jesus is our example. Jesus Christ desires that anyone who follows Him be a representative of what He stands for and an example to everyone they come in contact with; they bear the title of 'disciple of Jesus Christ.' A genuine disciple will be careful to follow those principles that will encourage others and cause them to see that it is possible to live for Christ in this present world. This is a primary way in doing ministry for the Lord—by the life you live (your lifestyle). It is the personal context of ministry—to be an example to people. Disciples of Jesus Christ can be role models to people they come in contact with in our homes, in the church, in the community, and at work. Your life can speak more loudly than what you say. It is all in what you do and not necessarily what you say! It is important to always be aware of how you operate in the world around you because it speaks loudly to your personal testimony and witness. For example, you wouldn't do the very things that you were delivered from. Again, it is all in the living it and doing it, rather than speaking it.

The other aspect of witness and testimony is when we are called to speak and to teach and to preach the good news of the gospel to people. This oral communication should be commensurate with the life you live. What you do and what you say both add to your overall message to people—that is a true testimony of the message of Jesus Christ in action.

Therefore, we must make a conscious effort to live out our testimony and witness to who we say we are—this is important! We should be encouragers—positive influencers—role models—living witnesses—a living testimony—a pattern for life—an example of standing firm in the faith in the midst of crises. We all can encourage one another in the faith of our Lord!

The Ministry Witness of Apostle Paul

On five different times, Paul explicitly tells other

Christians to "imitate me." This probably would be a big
challenge for many, but not Paul—Paul was completely
confident in his life in Christ until he invited all who would
listen to "imitate me" as I imitate Christ. Isn't that a
marvelous display of confidence in the life he now lived?
It wasn't him now, it was the Christ in him—"Christ in me
the hope of glory!" My, that should let you know that Paul
was not "ashamed of the gospel of Jesus Christ" and how
he was a living witness to that gospel. We also should be
like that in our Christian walk—our lives should be lived in
such a way as to invite others to Christ and to be a witness
and pattern of the truth of Christ until will want to
participate in this Kingdom and Kingdom work. What an
interchange! This is the Christian way! This is the way of
the Lord!

Paul commends the Church at Thessalonica not only
for imitating other churches, but also for serving as a
model themselves. Paul was advocating that churches and
Christians do both—be a model and also look to others
for a pattern. This can be a little "scary" in this day in
time—couldn't it?—when so many churches have not
been good examples or a good witness of discipleship on
the corporate or personal level.

Too many churches have turned to the "New Age
Doctrine"—redefining God and the Trinity—changing
wording in the hymns of the church—reinterpreting the
Bible, our Foundation of Truth—allowing erroneous
doctrine and teachings—allowing "same-sex marriage"—
the Bible is not the focal point any longer—grace is
redefined to mean anybody can be saved regardless to how
they live in this life—not good! This kind of church is not
what Jesus ordered for His church!

Imitate Christ

A Christian must first imitate Christ! When we imitate Christ, we can't go wrong. He is our chief pattern for living this life. He is the Foundation! Paul could boldly ask others to imitate him because (as a general rule), he was properly imitating the Lord Jesus Christ. Paul exhorts us to "imitate me, just as I also imitate Christ" (1 Cor 11:1, NKJV). He reminded the Thessalonians, "And you became followers (imitators) of us and the Lord" (1 Thess 1:6, NKJV). Therefore, Paul wanted others to imitate him as he imitated Christ, the Supreme Example.

Imitate Others

Although Christ is our supreme example, Paul also encourages us to look at other Christians as models, and some of them we find in Scriptures. It can be encouraging to the Body of Christ to view other churches and how they operate. Believers should realize that there are good and bad examples in the Scriptures. 1 Corinthians 10:11, for example, Paul mentions that concerning Israel's wandering in the wilderness—"Now all these things happened to them as examples, and they were written for our admonition, upon whom the ends of the ages have come." This warning was so we would not repeat their sins. Although some people stretch biblical models to justify their questionable actions, we should never do that. The Scriptures does contain inspired examples which we are to imitate and from which we should gain encouragement and instruction.

In addition to Scriptural models, we are encouraged by

Paul to look for models among believers today.

Imitate Me

Paul was not afraid to exhort others to imitate him as he imitated Christ. He wants each of us to live a life that is worthy of imitating—that is a positive influence on others. We must be imitations of Christ so others can imitate us.

I am challenged today to be a good example of what Christ wants me to be. I am also challenged to live a life that will be encouraging to others. Even on the social media, I am challenged to continue to use my writing skills and knowledge of the Word of God to encourage others. I encourage everyone as followers of Christ to be the disciple that Christ wants us to be. With this, the church can grow and prosper—the individual can grow and develop—other people can come to the knowledge of Jesus Christ! Amen.

SERMON 2 |
IT'S IN THE NAME OF JESUS:
SOME SPIRITUAL QUALITIES FOUND IN
THE NAME OF JESUS

Deliverance & Encouragement, Spiritual Growth & Development

Jesus took on the role of a servant (Phil 2:6-11). In the Greek the word for servant is *doulos*. The word actually means more than a slave or a minister. , servant means slave! Jesus became a slave for us—a bond slave. A bond slave was set free only when the conditions of bondage were met. Jesus was bound to die for our sins. Isn't that real love? He didn't have to do this, but His love was a deep love for humanity. The King of Kings would be a bond slave until that condition was met for our salvation and deliverance.

A bond slave was the lowest person in the "scale of servitude." Jesus humbled himself and took on the form of sinful flesh like a human being—just for us! Jesus was completely in the Father's will. John 13 describes a time when Jesus demonstrated His role as servant. He took the lowest servant role He could find by washing His disciples feet. This was the initial institution of the Sacrament of the church of "Feet Washing" that is practiced in some churches as a part of Holy Communion periodically.

Jesus gave up everything to come and die for our sins. His love for us and the Father was so great that nothing else mattered. He sacrificed His place in heaven. He became flesh with all its weaknesses, all its frailties except sin! There was no sin found in Him! He came to His own, and His own did not receive Him as the Messiah—the Savior of the world. They ridiculed Him! They rejected Him! They killed Him! He sacrificed Himself willingly so you and I could be forgiven, be given eternal life, be set free from the bondage of sin, and to be free to live for God.

God has exalted His name above all other names. We have no way to be forgiven but by that name—the power—and authority of Jesus. Every knee shall bow at the name of Jesus! This is a blessing and a warning. You can kneel to Jesus now or the day will come when you will bow before Him as your judge. We can accept Jesus as Lord and Savior, live for Him and glorify His name; or we can stand before Him at the judgment throne and bow in shame. We will bow before Him! His desire for us is to bow out of love and respect, not dishonor. He died to give us life!

At the name of Jesus, "If you have bowed to the name of Jesus as a born-again child of God, He has given you three gifts: strength, power, and hope. What's in the name of Jesus?

1. There is strength in the name of the Lord. Strength gives endurance. Strength that is not yours by nature, it is the strength of the living God who has come to dwell in you, strength to face crises when they come and not be destroyed—strength to endure! People of God can testify to the strength God has given when:

a. A parent stands by the bedside of a sick child
b. Tragedy strikes
c. Problems increase
d. Adversity strikes

Many of us have been there and the strength of the Lord took us through it. This strength gives us the energy to face life even when it is not going our way. This strength brings vigor, and vitality to life, and we experience the joy of living with Christ—abundant life! This strength provides us with courage—courage to face the enemy—courage to go through!

2. There is power in the name of the Lord. Power provides stamina—the ability to stand firm against Satan's storms and tragedies, the competence to say, "I can live for Jesus." "I do not have to fail." I can be faithful. "I can do all things through Christ that Strengthens me" (Philippians 4:13, NKJV). There is power in the name of Jesus! Through Jesus, I have the power of God (by His Holy Spirit), who loves me—the power of God to draw on! His power never runs out! I can have victory! Power provides control—where we have been slaves to our temptations and the lusts of the flesh, we now have control (power). We have the power to overcome temptation. We were slaves to sin, but now, we have been set free in the Power of the name Jesus!

3. There is hope in the name of the Lord. Hope gives you faith and trust for the future—hope gives you something:
a. To believe in—we can believe in the words of the

Lord. He will never tell us anything that is not true—neither will He lead us to fail.

b.   To trust in—When God tells us our sins are forgiven, we know He has forgiven our sins and has forgotten them. Nothing gives us more hope than knowing God has forgiven and forgotten our sins. Because of Jesus' death on the cross, our sins were carried away.

c.   To give us promise—we have the promise of a new beginning—the promise of a life full of possibilities—the promise of a secure future. Acts 2:21 says, "And it shall come to pass that whoever calls on the name of the Lord shall be saved." (NKJV) When you are saved God gives you strength—power—and hope all in the name of the Lord! That covers the total man! All that we need is in the name of Jesus our Lord!

It's in the name of Jesus—our inner power, strength, and hope—also those things that causes external problems as well. We are covered inside and out! It's all in the name of Jesus: power, strength, hope, salvation, blessings, life, deliverance, happiness, joy, peace, healing, stability, control, endurance, and much more! Just acknowledge Jesus by accepting Him as your personal Savior and Lord; and He will give you everything you need! These are the spiritual qualities found in the name of Jesus. In fact, His name means deliverance and complete salvation; inner and outer peace—our Lord and Savior! Acknowledge Him and He will give you the desires of your heart!

SERMON 3 |
THE FOLLOWERS OF CHRIST

Matthew 28:16-20
(16) Then the eleven disciples went to Galilee, to the mountain
where Jesus had told them to go. (17) When they saw Him, they
worshiped Him; but some doubted. (18) Then Jesus came to
them and said, "All authority in heaven and on earth has been
given to me. (19) Therefore go and make disciples of all nations,
baptizing them in the name of the Father and of the Son and of
the Holy Spirit, (20) and teaching them to obey everything I have
commanded you. And surely I am with you always, to the very
end of the age."

Disciples are People of Purpose

The followers of Christ are His disciples. Specifically,
Christ's inner circle consisted of the twelve men who He
chose to follow Him in performing ministry wherever He
went—these men were His ministry team. His first
disciples were Simon Peter and his brother Andrew; James
son of Zebedee, and his brother John; Philip and
Bartholomew; Thomas and Matthew the tax collector;
James son of Alphaeus, and Thaddaeus; Simon the Zealot
and Judas Iscariot, who betrayed Him. After Jesus was
betrayed by Judas Iscariot, Acts 1:15-26 references the
addition of Matthias—making the number of the inner
circle twelve again. That is a significant number since He
was intent on keeping the number at twelve. In this inner
circle of disciples, there was a cross-section of men with
differing trades that probably gave Christ a contrasting
group of men. However; besides the ministry team

everyone who is a follower of Christ is considered a disciple of Jesus Christ, even to those of us today. These are people who honor Him as the Messiah, follow His principles and lead others to Jesus Christ.

People in Christian ministry are people who are willing to help people who are in need. Your purpose is to put your particular God-given talents, knowledge, skills, experiences, and positions in life to use in specific ways. No one person no matter how gifted can do everything. Jesus knew His purpose. He said, "I am come to seek and save the lost," (Lk 19:10). In John 10:10, He says, "I am come that they might have life and that more abundantly." Our purpose should be in line with Jesus' purpose. After all, we are His followers. He further says, "The Spirit of the Lord is upon me and has anointed me to preach the Gospel" (Lk 4:18). Jesus fulfilled His purpose; He concentrated on teaching, preaching, healing (both physical and spiritual). Matthew 9:35-38 says:

> *(35) Jesus went through all the towns and villages, teaching in their synagogues, preaching the "good news of the kingdom and healing every disease and sickness. (36) When he saw the crowds, he had compassion on them, because they were harassed and helpless, like sheep without a shepherd. (37) Then he said to his disciples, "The harvest is plentiful but the workers are few. (38) ask the Lord of the harvest, therefore, to send out workers into his harvest field."*

People who follow Him participate in Jesus' purpose for ministry to spread the gospel to reach men and women for Christ. That is a real disciple of Jesus Christ. His people must be willing to work for Him in the work of ministry.

Almost 2000 years after His death, over one billion

people have faith in Christ as their Savior, Lord, and Master. Followers of Christ always ask the question—like Apostle Paul (Acts 9:6, KJV)—"Lord, what do you want me to do?" Upon hearing Christ's answer to this question, we give the Lord's will priority in our lives. The "followers of Christ" know their purpose in Kingdom work—and that is to work the work of Him who sent us while it is day.

Disciples are People of Preparation

To be a follower of Christ, there are at least two kinds of preparation necessary for effectiveness in Christian ministry. The first kind is Spiritual preparation. It is already an established fact that in order to engage in Christian ministry, one must be a follower of Christ—a believer. So, spiritual preparation has to do with spiritual growth and spiritual maturity. We must be constantly developing a more intimate relationship between our spirits and the Spirit of God! Christian ministry is spiritual work, whether it is preaching the Gospel or sheltering the homeless or other church programs. It is spiritual work! Whatever kind of ministry we do, it is to be done with an attitude of love, compassion, and humility. Spiritual growth takes place through public and private prayer, scripture reading, study, Christian fellowship, worship, and praise in order for us to develop the proper attitude to do effective ministry for Jesus Christ.

The second kind of preparation is of the mind and body. It involves the fullest possible development of our God-given gifts. The Lord gives us eyesight but He will not teach us to read; we must apply ourselves in perfecting the gifts that God gave us. The Lord gives us mental capacity—a mind—but we must actively seek, apprehend, and learn. For instance, the Lord gives us the gift of music and artistic ability, but we must practice to develop them. The Lord gives us messages, but we must prepare it for presentation to the "glory of God."

The Bible says in Luke 2:52, "And Jesus increased in wisdom and stature and in favor with God and man." Jesus, our Savior, had to increase to develop, to prepare to carry out His mission. He spent 30 years, preparing for three years of public ministry. Jesus had to prepare for a mammoth job. He spent 10 years getting ready for every one year He ministered. Now, isn't that something? Young men and women today don't want to spend any time in preparation for ministry—they want to start the "business" right away—giving themselves titles… prophet, apostle, bishop, arch-bishop, pastor, evangelist, and still don't know much about the scriptures, about leadership, or how to relate to people. There is no desire to be under leadership or mentorship. There is no desire to be subject to leadership whatsoever. In order to do the work of the Lord effectively, one must study, follow leadership, and accept mentorship. They think they know it all! In fact, there should be a period of waiting. Jesus wants us to know that the first call to minister is the call to prepare. Effective ministry is a reflection of effective preparation.

Disciples are People of Patience

Patience is a fruit of the Spirit. Job displayed great patience in waiting until his change came. He had gone through the loss of his wife, his children, his cattle and flock, his land and was facing death. He had lost everything. But, in the end, he received double and more for all that he had lost. Job is our chief model of patience. Patience is one of the minister's most prized possessions. Patience is important because, through it we learn some strategic lessons. Patience facilitates the learning process. We learn about God, others, and ourselves.

In the process of being patient, we learn how strong and how weak we are. We learn we are stronger in some areas than we thought, and weaker in some other areas. Patience teaches us confidence and humility. I do not believe that Job could have imagined himself coming as close as he did to absolute despair. But he stood up under the weight and pressure. The Job that emerged in chapter 42 was richer in humility and wisdom.

Disciples are People of Partnership

Jesus, the Son of God, refused to go out ministering alone. One of the first things that He did was to recruit disciples to work with Him. His disciples became effective Christian ministers because they followed Christ and learned from Him. Peter preached one sermon and 3000 people were saved and another 2000 added shortly after that (Acts 2:41, 4:4). His disciples were valuable to the up-building of the Kingdom of God. The learned from Jesus and felt His passion for ministry. A mighty army was formed. We are also soldiers in the Army of the Lord today. As His followers, we are warriors for God. Disciples work together to achieve the work of the kingdom of God.

Disciples are People of Spiritual Warfare in the Army of the Lord

The Disciples of Christ are constantly engaged in spiritual warfare. Disciples must always be willing to fight for the cause of Christ. It is warfare of the spirit, not against flesh and blood, but spiritual wickedness in heavenly places. Our dedication as a follower of Christ must be a solid commitment. Our resolve should be sure and firm!

I remember my experience as a soldier in the army of the United States of America. I had basic training in Fort Benning, Georgia—commonly called "boot camp." For 10 weeks, I had intense training in hand to hand combat, physical training, weapons training, etc. We even wore uniforms to look the part of a soldier. We trained in every area that would make us ready to serve in the military during the Vietnam Era war. Just like that training, there are preparations and training that must be made in entering the Army of the Lord. For the followers of Christ, the training and preparations are *spiritual*!

The Warfare of Spirit-filled Believers

Ephesians chapter 6 gives the information that the Disciple of Christ needs to be aware of for engaging in spiritual warfare as a follower of Christ:

a. The warrior's power comes from God. Verse 10 reads, "Finally, be strong in the Lord and in His Mighty Power."

b. The warrior's armor is Spiritual. Verse 11: "Put on the full armor of God so that you can take your stand against the devil's schemes."

c. The warrior's foes are spiritual forces of evil. Verse 12: "For our struggle is not against flesh and blood, but against the rulers, against the authorities, against the powers of this dark world and against the spiritual forces of evil in the heavenly realms."

d. The warrior's uniform Spiritual covering. Verses 13-17: "Put on the whole armor of God, so that when the day of evil comes, you may be able to stand your ground, and after you have done everything, to stand. Stand firm with the belt of truth buckled around the waist, with the breastplate of righteousness in place, and with the feet fitted with gospel of peace. In addition, take up the shield of faith, for extinguishing the flashing arrows or "fiery darts" of the evil one. Put on the helmet of salvation and the sword of the Spirit, which is the Word of God." A warrior-disciple is fully clothed with spiritual armor. Fully protected! You need the Spirit of God in our lives at all times in order to be able to stand up against the evil one.

e. The warrior's resource is prayer. The Bible declares that man should always pray and not faint. Prayer is our chief weapon. Verse 18: "And pray in the Spirit on all occasions—at every opportunity—with all kinds of prayers and requests." With this in mind, be alert and always continue praying for the saints. Prayer is the key to activating our spiritual armor and being fully prepared for battle with the enemy. Paul continued his emphasis on the importance of prayer in verses 19 and 20 when he requested prayer for himself that he would be able to stand firm and speak fearlessly with words that would enable him to share the mysteries of the gospel message, even as an "ambassador in chains." No disciple is exempt from praying for victory in Jesus. That's what makes a good soldier—a good warrior—remaining constant in prayer!

Are you a soldier in the Army of the Lord? Are you willing to fight the good fight of faith? Are you willing to maintain your status as a follower of Jesus Christ?

SERMON 4 |
THE MARKS OF A PERSONAL RELATIONSHIP WITH GOD

Christian Growth & Development

A relationship with God has many of the same characteristics that mark a personal relationship between two friends. These factors include some degree of:

a.   Mutual recognition—each knows the other.
b.   Mutual openness—each approaches the other.
c.   Mutual interests—each shares with the other.
d.   Mutual respect—each honors the other.

Such a relationship means more than knowing of or about someone. We might say that we know the president of the United States. But if the president can't pick us out of a crowd, if we can't get access to him, or if he has never shared our thoughts, or if he has never shared our feelings, or if he has never shared our decisions, then we are claiming a friendship we don't really have. We don't really know him; there is no relationship. This example could be applied to anyone. You cannot claim to know someone in the real sense of the word if there is no background, no history, between you and another.

A relationship with God is similar. If our friendship is real, we will welcome God into our lives and affairs. Our actions and ways will show we believe we want Him in our homes, in our plans, in our laughter, and in our tears. Let's take a closer look at the six marks of a personal relationship with God.

1 • A Spiritual Relationship with God

To be a friend of our Lord, there must be a spiritual relationship with Him. This gives us an insight into the spiritual nature of God—a more intimate look into Who He is—a relationship of worship and praise. We can be in tune with the Almighty God through a relationship of unity and fellowship with our God. There is a chasing after the things of God and a closeness that we can only have through constant fellowship with Him in the sanctuary. Since He is holy, we also strive to be holy. We can relate to God in all His creation; we can see Him in nature and in the elements, in the beauty of His creation. We acknowledge that He is God and there is none other but Him. Yes, we worship Him in the beauty of holiness and in His supreme majesty. Lord God, we honor You above all the earth.

The Psalmist even cried out to the Lord and sang the songs of Zion! He said I will extol thee and bless His holy name in all the earth. He consistently humbled himself in praise to the Lord of Lords and the King of Kings! He declared that the Lord God was his fortress, his strong tower, his deliverer, his hope in battle, his buckler, and strength. Honor the Lord and praise Him as your Lord and Savior! Declare your honor love for the Lord! I declare that He will be your Lord and we shall be His people says the Lord. Let's get personal with God and stay in His presence constantly in communion and fellowship with Him.

2 • A Christ-Centered Relationship with God Is Necessary

According to the Bible, not only is a personal relationship with God a spiritual relationship, but it is also a Christ-centered relationship. Jesus Christ is our mediator, the only begotten Son of the Living God. He is our Sacrificial Lamb—the one who redeemed us from a world of sinfulness. Jesus is that member of the Godhead that willingly came all the way from heaven down to earth to redeem man, displaying His loving nature. He loved us so much until He took the pain and suffering for us—by breaking into history as the Jesus of history and the Christ of faith.

We relate to Him in that while we were yet sinners, He died for us. He didn't have to do it, but He did. The more we think about that the more we relate to His love for us. We have to remember that He loved us and loves us! We also can increase our relationship with Christ by continuously meditating on the Foundation of Truth which is the Word of God. The more we study the word, the more we learn about Him and will relate to Him. His words are power! His words are life! His words are strength! His words are love! Do you love Christ?

We also can have a more Christ-centered relationship with God by relating to His activity in the world today! We know that in the biblical times, He went around doing good works and healing the sick, raising the dead, restoring sight to the blind, and stopped bleeding sores. We know of His works; we know of His deeds; we know of His acts of love. Knowing these things will increase our relationship with Him.

Further, we know Him as the wise teacher who loved deeply, fed thousands of people, working miracle after miracle. We also know He lived a sinless life, He fulfilled Old Testament prophecy, claimed to be the promised Messiah, and gave Himself to secure our forgiveness of sins for everyone who would trust Him. It was Jesus who said, "He who has seen Me has also seen the Father" (John 14:9).

Jesus Christ is our mediator, and mediators often play an important role in helping to resolve family, labor, and legal disputes. When emotions flare, insight is lost, communication stops, and stubbornness sets in. In such instances, an arbitrator can often bring renewed perspective and a plan for resolution. That's what Jesus is—our mediator between us and God. Everything we know of God and everything we need from Him is deeply affected by our attitude toward Christ. He said, when you have seen me, you have also seen the Father. I am your mediator! I love you!

The apostle Paul understood the necessity of a Christ-centered relationship with God. In 1 Corinthians 1:1-9, He made it clear that He was not promoting a system of ideas. He was speaking of a relationship with God based on:

CHRIST whom we serve (verse 1)
CHRIST who sets Christians a part (verse 2)
CHRIST on whose name Christians call in the time of need (verse 2)
CHRIST who is our Lord (verse 2)
CHRIST who gives us grace and peace (verse 3)
CHRIST who brought us the grace of God (verse 4)

CHRIST who has enriched us in every way (verse 5)

CHRIST who is confirmed by the testimony or
experience of Him in us (verse 6)

CHRIST for whom we eagerly wait for the revelation
of Him (verse 7)

CHRIST who will keep us to the end (verse 8)

CHRIST who will have His day (verse 8)

CHRIST to whom God has joined us together in unity
(verse 9)

Jesus Christ received is holiness begun! Jesus Christ cherished is holiness advancing! And Jesus Christ received is holiness complete! Complete salvation!

There is no question that a personal relationship with God must be a Christ-centered relationship. It is Christ and Christ alone who can bring us to God and cleanse us from the pollution of the world, and be our ever present source of life and help. It is Christ, the living word, who reveals, defines, and expresses the personality of the Father. It is Christ who should continually be in our thoughts as Lord and life. It is Christ, who, by His Spirit, is a constant presence in and with all who have put their faith in Him.

3 • A Obedient Relationship with God Is Necessary

Any husband who is content to be just "one of the boys" in his wife's eyes isn't much of a husband and the relationship is nonexistent. And the same holds true for a wife who is content with a husband just being blasé with her. There is no relationship at all. A healthy relationship is centered on a mutual submission of the two parties involved, and I did say two parties. A woman doesn't want to be treated just like "one of the girls"—she is not content with that. The intimacy of a marriage relationship carries with it a great sense of mutual commitment that will have a bearing on all of the couple's other activities and relationships—the wife comes first. The husband comes first.

A relationship with God begins with a fear/awe that will drive us to the safety, certainty, and enjoyment of His love. We should reverence and stand in awe of the greatness of God! Along with David, we can say, "I sought the Lord, and He heard me, and delivered me from all my fears." (Ps 34:4, NKJV) And David added, "The angel of the Lord encamps around those who fear Him, and delivers them. Oh, taste and see that the Lord is good; blessed is the man who trusts in Him! Oh, fear the Lord, you His saints! There is no want to those who fear Him" (Ps 34:7-9, NKJV). That type of statement comes from someone who knew God personally. It comes from someone who personally experienced God.

God is to be trusted, and obeyed more than all others. Obedience like reverence (awe, fear) is something we tend to resist. Obedience is a way of showing that we really do know the Lord and that we are growing in our knowledge of how good, loving, and wise He is. Apostle John wrote:

1 John 2:3-6
(3) "Now by this we know that we know Him, if we keep His commandments. (4) He who says, "I know Him," and does not keep His commandments, is a liar, and the truth is not in Him. (5) But whoever keeps His word, truly the love of God is perfected in Him. By this we know that we are in Him. (6) He

who says he abides in Him ought himself also to walk just as He walked. (NKJV)

Those who abide in Christ ought to walk just as He walked—that is in unity and harmony. That's the way it is in developing a personal relationship with God through His Son Jesus Christ—to walk as He walked in fellowship with Him.

The fear, trust, and obedience involved in knowing the Lord do not leave us the way we were. They make us better because Christ lives within. They change us until this relationship possesses us and dominates us—bringing us heart to heart and face to face with the God of all goodness and light.

4 • A Mutually-Felt Relationship Is Required (James 4:7-10)

Our relationship with one another can only be as strong as our relationship to God. A mutually-felt relationship is a love relationship on either level. Some people when thinking about God see Him as far away from us. They long for assurance that God would smile on them and move toward them. But they assume Him to be too selective to feel anything for them. Some people even see Him as an unchanging, eternal spirit who lives far above the ever-changing winds of pain and emotion that blow in and out of our lives.

But this is not true. Our God of the Scriptures assure us that He feels deeply for the most broken, dejected, oppressed, and hurting people. He is touched by our weakness! God relates to his people personally and presently in a very intimate way. He rejoices with us when we are happy, sorrows when we are sad, and grieves when we sin.

God is vulnerable to all of our needs. He has exposed His own heart to all of the loveless and heartless things that we do to Him. The Bible tells us that God can be: Pleased (Heb 11:5); grieved and sorrowful (Gen 6:6; Eph 4:30-32); provoked and tested (Ps 78:40-41); burdened and wearied (Isa 43:24); angered, agitated, and furious (Ezek 16:42-43). God can feel all these emotions at the same time if necessary. He can also feel our infirmities!

Specifically, Ephesians 4:30-32 says, "Do not grieve the Holy Spirit of God, by whom you were sealed for the day of redemption. Let all bitterness, wrath, anger, clamor, and evil speaking be put away from you, with all malice. And be kind to one another, tenderhearted, forgiving one another, even as God in Christ forgave you" (NKJV). We must exemplify the same qualities that God displays to each of us. This is how we feel the pains of others through our relationship with Christ!

The greatest evidence of God's decision to make Himself vulnerable to us is found in the pains and suffering of Christ who revealed the Father to us. In the face of Jesus Christ, we find the face of God. Jesus is the one who suffered for us so He could bring us to the Father. God loves us that much! God is able to relate intimately to all of us at the same time as He desires. God knows you—and you must get to know Him. God loves us—and you must love Him. A relationship must be mutual!

To develop a personal relationship with God means to learn to love what He loves and hate what He hates. To know God is to be affected by Him. No one can know God without being changed by Him. Anyone who comes into God's presence will be changed and touched by the one who loves us to the utmost.

James 4:7-10
> *(7) Therefore, submit to God. Resist the devil and he will flee from you. (8) Draw near to God and He will draw neat to you. Cleanse your hands, you sinners; and purify your hearts, you double-minded. (9) Lament and mourn and weep! Let your laughter be turned to mourning and your joy to gloom. (10) Humble yourselves in the sight of the Lord, and He will lift you up. (NKJV)*

To know God in this way means allowing our hearts to be broken by the things that breaks His heart. It means finding joy in the things that bring Him joy, discovering strength in His strength, and receiving hope in the assurance that nothing is too hard for Him. It means finding a new lease on life in one who offers us forgiveness in exchange for our repentance, comfort in trade for our sorrow, and the promise of a world to come for our willingness to release our grip on this present world.

We are changed as we discover that to know God is to love Him. To love Him is to give Him first place in our hearts. Giving Him first place to care about those He cares about, to love what He loves, to hate what He hates, and to join Him in the family business of redeeming broken lives. This is the kind of healthy relationship God calls us to. We must grow to know God better and to cherish Him more.

5 • A Growing Relationship with God

To continue to grow your relationship with God is to continue to live for Him in your daily lives. To continue to grow your relationship with God is to continue to study His word. To continue to grow your relationship with God is to continue to practice His principles. To continue to grow and become more personal with the Lord is to continue to worship Him and praise Him in the sanctuary and at all times. To become closer to God is to love Him more and to push His agenda even when it may not be popular. We must stand up for Him at all times! Stay in mutual fellowship and communion with Him. Everyday should be a closer walk with God. Allow the Holy Spirit to infuse you with God's power.

No one who calls the Lord God as their Savior should work contrary to the way that God has laid out for His people. There has to be unity, harmony, and fellowship. Nothing has changed about this; even in this century, God will be God—He never changes. Certainly the world around us has changed; some changes were good changes for the betterment of mankind. But there are changes that are not good: reinventing His word (The Bible), reinterpreting His message, altering the personality (character) of God, redefining what God's church should be about, a changing of God's ideas about what is right and what is wrong, a redefining of what is marriage, and the list goes on and on. God never intended for these nor other things to change. Instead of getting closer to God, many people are moving farther apart from Him. Now is the time for moving closer to God and not separating from Him. There are so many questions—so many changes in the world and people need to get closer to God, especially those of the Household of Faith!

The distortion of the truth, living contradictory lives, etc. is very misleading. Being a Christian, loving God, yet your life shows something differently—this can cause people to become alienated from God instead of getting closer to Him.

Every believer has as a goal to move people closer to God and to grow spiritually. This is where our blessings lie, in staying close to God and doing His will. This closer and more personal relationship can grow through attending worship services, praising God as a habit—including prayer and fasting. Remember the characteristics of the New Testament church formed in the book of Acts of the Apostles… The revival fire and flame must never go out! Revival is the key to continued spiritual vitality.

6 • A Sharing Relationship with God's People

God desires for believers to encourage one another through a ministry of reconciliation to continue in the faith. Also, believers should have a heart for the needs of people who may be suffering various needs in their lives. This is the way God intended it to be because as we help others, we also help ourselves; it is an interchange between the brotherhood. The people who are non-churched and who don't know the Lord as their Savior must be able to see the difference between a believer and a non-believer—between those who are disciples of Christ and those who are not. We are a sharing community of faith—the *koinonia*—a body of believers who are in fellowship. The koinonia displays the Spirit of God within us to all of mankind—a lost world. We must encourage one another to stay with God, get closer to Him, and make every effort to grow in our personal relationship with God! The greatest witness of a personal relationship with God is in how we relate to our fellow man. This is the proof! You cannot say you love God who you have never seen and not love your brothers and sisters who you see everyday—some of which you even worship with every Sunday. We have to express and share the love we say we have for God with people. We are an extension of God in this present world to be a witness, example, an ambassador to the people of the world. Through the love that God has shown us, then, we must share with others so that people can see the love of God being manifested in the lives of those who say that they are followers of Christ. Be consistent in your life in Christ. Let the world see Christ operating within us. This will glorify the father who is in heaven! To get even closer and more personal with god is to love, fellowship, and get closer to the people of God! A friendship with Jesus is a friendship with God and people. "He that loves me shall be loved of my Father, and I will love Him" (John 14:21).

Friendship with Jesus (traditional hymn)

1. *A friend of Jesus O what bless that one so weak as I should ever have a friend like this to lead me to the sky.*
CHORUS: *Friendship with Jesus, Fellowship divine; O what blessed sweet communion, Jesus is a friend of mine.*
2. *A friend when other friendships cease, A friend when others fail; A friend who gives me joy and peace, A friend who will prevail.* (CHORUS)

3. *A friend to lead me in the dark, A friend who knows the way; A friend to steer my weak, frail bark, A friend my debts to pay.* (CHORUS)

4. *A friend when sickness lays me low, A friend when death draws near; A friend as through the vale I go, A friend too help and cheer.* (CHORUS)

5. *A friend when life's rough voyage is o'er, A friend when death is past. A friend to greet on Heaven's shore, A friend when home at last.* (CHORUS) *Friendship with Jesus, Fellowship divine; O what blessed sweet communion, Jesus is a friend of mine!*

Leaning on the Everlasting Arms by Anthony J. Showalter (public domain)

What a fellowship, what a joy divine, leaning on the everlasting arms; what blessedness, what a peace is mine, Leaning on the everlasting arms. Chorus: Leaning, leaning, safe and secure from all alarms; Leaning, leaning, leaning on the everlasting arms.

O how sweet to walk in this pilgrim way, leaning on the everlasting arms, O how height the path grows from day to day, leaning on the everlasting arms. Chorus: Leaning, leaning, Safe and secure from all alarms; Leaning, leaning, Leaning on the everlasting arms.

What have I to dread, what have I to fear, leaning on the everlasting arms? I have blessed peace with my Lord so near, leaning on the everlasting arms. Chorus: Leaning, leaning, Safe and secure from all alarms; Leaning, leaning, Leaning on the everlasting arms.

THE WORKMANSHIP OF CHRIST

Day 1

CHRIST, HEAD OF THE CHURCH

Ephesians 1:21-23
(21) Far above all rule and authority, power and dominion, and every title that can be given, not only in the present age but also in the one to come. (22) And God placed all things under his feet and appointed him to be head over everything for the church, (23) which is his body, the fullness of him who fills everything in every way.

The church is in an important position in the world. Since its inception, it has been placed in high regard, as it was instituted by God and placed in the hands of Christ to be the head of it. Regardless of the problems of the church, it is nevertheless the complement to Jesus Christ and is responsible for carrying out His mandate to be the visible witness of Himself to all people. Working in cooperation with Jesus Christ is a position of honor and should be displayed as such.

As members of Christ's church, He expects you to strive for perfection and true holiness. Be the example Christ wants you to be. He has equipped you with His Holy Spirit to empower you and assist you in living out His principles. The Lord has given various gifts of the Spirit to the Body of Christ that provides us with a support system helping us be the true witnesses and examples of His church. Know that the Holy Spirit propels you to function effectively. Give glory to the Father and to our Lord and Savior! Remember that we are His workmanship and are spiritually connected to Him. He is our Creator, our Lawgiver, the Forgiver of our sins, the Dispenser of

His Spirit, the Giver of eternal life, and our Guide through life who is our chief example of holiness.

Day 2

TRUE BELIEVERS ARE ONE WITH CHRIST

Galatians 3:27-28
> *(27) For all of you who were baptized into Christ have clothed yourselves with Christ. (28) There is neither Jew nor Greek, slave nor free, male nor female, for you are all one in Christ Jesus.*

As a true believer, you are clothed with Jesus Christ! You are one (in unity) with Christ! God gives you His Spirit in the inward parts of you, but then it is your responsibility to nourish and nurture that Spirit within you through prayer, communion, fellowship with the church, studying the Word of God, and keeping your soul fed with wholesome things. You must be extra mindful of how you live your life because you now belong to Christ. You are a portrait of Christ! You are created in His image and likeness! You are submerged in Christ!

The power of Jesus Christ should manifest in your daily life, whether it is your conduct, your attitude, your witness, or your testimony. He must be a part of your heart, mind, soul, and spirit! Since Jesus Christ by His Spirit abides within you, you are a new person—a new creation! You have put on Christ and are in Him and His love.

Day 3

YOUR ABUNDANT BLESSINGS ARE ON THE WAY

1 Kings 18:41
> *And Elijah said to Ahab, "Go, eat and drink, for there is the sound of a heavy rain."*

Trust in the Lord and He will produce whatever you need to sustain you. It may seem like nothing is going to happen positively for you, but God will always provide an inkling of a blessing to boost your faith enough for you to know that more is coming!

The verse states, "Go, eat and drink…" Do not worry any longer. Meaning, do not lose any sleep, do not toil over a situation, do not try to work it out for yourself (outside of God's will and timing), and do not doubt God. He will bring it to pass.

I have noticed in my past experiences that problems that seem insurmountable were always worked out in one way or another. After you've done all you can do in your own power, then leave it alone and rest. God will grant you peace in the storms of life!

There was a drought in Elijah's land because of the evil that King Ahab, king of Israel, had spread throughout the land in terms of widespread idolatry and all kinds of ungodly activities. God then said that that is enough; Elijah was instructed to announce that rain was on the way. Mind you, it wasn't raining yet, but Elijah had seen an inkling of the blessing coming to pass. The ground was barren and parched, and there were no noticeable signs of rain. But, when God says *'enough!'* He will act on our behalf!

In this day in time, there is much evil and disrespect of God and His word. There will come a time when God says enough. In the meantime, just leave every situation to God. Trust and wait on Him and the blessing will be on the way. There's a sound of heavy rain coming…

Day 4

REFLECTIONS: ADVICE FROM THE HEART OF A PASTOR ON DISTRACTIONS AND PROCRASTINATION

I must admit that I have had problems with procrastination. I would do research papers a day before they were due—making "As"—but running everyone around me "crazy." Situations like this could wreak havoc on the body. I remember I had to preach my first sermon in a homiletics class. What I wrote was incomplete, but I went in anyway—sweating. My professor, Dr. Isaac R. Clarke, stopped me right at the point where I had stopped writing…Whew!!! My wife almost took me to the ER, but called a church for prayer. Many are last minute people, but this can be counterproductive. Thank God, I have learned better!

Never put off 'til tomorrow what you can do today. I try to teach this to everyone who will listen. Sometimes, I think that some pastors wait until they get to the pulpit to preach a message; the pastor is now ill prepared (often rambling on random topics), and the sermon is not covered in prayer beforehand. I've heard it said before, 'Open your mouth and the Lord will speak for you,' but studying is key in showing yourself approved unto God. Some also pray to the Lord to pass examinations, but haven't studied. He will speak through you and bring knowledge back to your remembrance when you have studied. God doesn't cheat for anyone. He requires honesty and integrity.

Distractions and procrastination are two impediments to progress and moving ahead to reach your goals. Distractions are mostly from outside forces, but procrastination is mostly from within oneself. With the Holy Spirit, determination, and focus these two hindrances are defeated. You will have the power to achieve. Make preparation before mounting that sacred stage, or *any* stage of life.

Day 5

A COVENANT RELATIONSHIP WITH GOD

God made a covenant relationship with His creation. Follow through on your end; come into agreement with the Lord. In this we learn how to live in this life. You will find that this commitment will enhance your human relationships as well. You will be able to make covenant relationships with your family and friends. Consider the following passage:

Num 25:13
He and his descendants will have a covenant of a lasting

priesthood, because he was zealous for the honor of his God and made atonement for the Israelites.

Let it be known that God loves you to the utmost and wants you to love Him back. You love Him by making a commitment to Him and striving to live for Him every day. God accepts us as His sons and daughters. He wants the best for us. God displays His love for each of us as if we are his only child.

There is tremendous temptation in the world that would cause many to turn their attention away from God. But, always be reminded of the supreme love and sacrifice that God made for you.

The context of chapter 25 lets us know that the situation had become very grave for the Israelite men as they succumbed to the evil seduction of the Midianite women. Seductions could come to us today in terms of the diabolical plots of Satan to entice us and cause us to forget God—greed, lusts of the flesh, selfishness, etc. Do not be seduced by the things of this world, but rather stay close to God. Do not be distracted by the activities of the world. The chapter's context further shows that the Midianite women were tricking the Israelites into committing idolatry—blatantly turning away from God. So God started a plague that threatened to wipe out the entire camp. In the above verse 15, there is a covenant made describing the blessings of the zealous—those committed to honoring God. God has said in His word that He is a jealous God and will have no other gods before Him. Trust God and live an abundant life in Him.

Day 6

THE IMPORTANCE OF SEEKING GOD

Amos 5:14
> *Seek good, not evil,*
> *That you may live.*
> *Then the Lord God Almighty will be with you,*
> *Just as you say He is.*

God is not lost. *We* are in a lost condition until we find Him. To seek means to turn to God in trust and confidence. In Amos 5:14, "seeking" and "living" are in the imperative; it is a command to seek God. Seek, in this case, does not mean to search for something that is lost, but rather to run after something in longing—to desire goodness instead of evil. God is right before us and all we have to do is simply come to His throne with an open and willing heart and mind, and God will be there with us.

Seeking God does not mean to get something from Him, but to seek God for what He. According to the Word of God, if we do this, then we will live forever in eternity. The word "live" in this context means to live abundantly and eternally. You cannot get this type of happiness from material goods or relationships only, but God will bless you with genuine abundant living that can never be measured in terms of material goods. God's abundance is complete and fulfilling. So, living the life of abundance is connected to your relationship with Him! Seek God and live!

Day 7

A PROPHETIC WORD

Revelation 6:15
> *Then the kings of the earth, the princes, the generals, the rich, the mighty, and every slave and every free man hid in caves and among the rocks of the mountains.*

Satan is allowed to rule the natural earth for a season, but God is in complete control of everything—the natural and the spiritual worlds. There will come a time when God through His Son, Jesus Christ, will return to openly wage war against the powers of darkness. The powers that be are seemingly in control right now, influencing the agendas for the current age concerning the rich and the poor; the slave and the free; the high and the low. There will come a time when all of Satan's imps will scatter and flee to the caves and mountains, fleeing the wrath of the Lord! Remember the account of Noah and the flood where the people were held accountable for their deeds.

There are signs of the times now that people ignore. The powers that be are busying themselves at this time in trying to dispel, overlook, and ignore the signs of the times; but, there will come a time when they *cannot* be ignored! Their dismissal will not work in the coming of The Day of the Lord. Be ready when He comes!

Day 8

DEVOTION

Acts 2:41-42

(41) Those who accepted his message were baptized, and about three thousand were added to their number that day. (42) They devoted themselves to the apostles' teaching and to the fellowship, to the breaking of bread and to prayer.

There was a time, signified by this day of Pentecost, when the church was unified—perhaps as unified as it ever was in its entire history. Those verses reveal two elements of the time when the unity of the church was at its very peak.

1) The first-century church was devoted to the apostles' doctrine. In the first century the doctrine, or teaching, was "the faith once delivered." The church was steadfast in this teaching. They were firm. They were single-minded. They were determined in learning and of following it. They did not drift. They did not swerve from doctrine, and it produced what it is supposed to: faith—in God, God's way, and confidence and trust in putting these things into practice. Different views tried creeping in as Paul's writings attest to, but the church remained deeply convicted.

2) They took care of each other. They were very much concerned for their brother's welfare. They sold all their goods and turned them over to the administration of the church to distribute equally to all. Some interpret this as

communism, but it was not communism; no lives were taken and goods were not taken by force. They willingly gave up their possessions out of the goodness of their own heart. The church voluntarily looked out for each other, striving to meet each other's needs. As servants. The church said amen.

Day 9

STAND UP AND FIGHT THE SPIRIT OF BAAL

A passage of scripture in 1 Kings 18:16-40 gives an account of Elijah as he confronted the 450 prophets of Baal. He stood up to them on Mount Carmel and defeated them because of the power that he received from the Lord.

That is an excellent example of how you as a child of God can stand up to the spirit of Baal today. Fight, defend, and win against whatever obstacles placed before you, follower of God. In this day in time the challenge of Satan befalls Christians and the churches of God. Satan is moving forward with his agenda and dishearteningly it often appears that he is winning a battle in the war on morality. It is appalling that every day something new happens to give Satan a little progress in pushing his agenda. What is more appalling is how many unconcerned attitudes there are among today's churches and among ministry leaders/pastors. A great number of them stand idly by while Satan is perpetrating on our families, children, communities, schools, and even churches. Many pastors, ministry leaders, and churches are content with preaching a soft and tolerating "gospel." Prosperity and motivational messages are the order of the day. Many of them never speak of removing sin or on combating the true evils, immorality, and corrupt trends of this day. Churches and leaders are content with pushing the church as just another business venture for monetary gains and lusts of the flesh. Some are essentially aiding and abetting Satan's program while ignoring the program of God for which we are called to preach. It is time to stop allowing the devil to have his way and to commit ourselves to preaching the gospel as it should be preached according to the foundation of truth—the Bible. There is too much compromise and disrespect to the house of God—too much fighting against the principles of God's Word! There is too much compromise! It is either God's way or Satan's way. Which way do *you* choose?

Day 10

GROW IN GRACE AND POWER

Hebrews 5:12-14

(12) In fact, though by this time you ought to be teachers, you need someone to teach you the elementary truths of God's word all over again. You need milk, not solid food! (13) Anyone who lives on milk, being still an infant, is not acquainted with the teaching about righteousness. (14) But solid food is for the mature, who by constant use have trained themselves to distinguish good from evil.

It is time to be weaned from milk, and receive the solid food of the gospel. Will you remain children forever? Or will you 'grow in grace' and in the power of God?

The people spoken to in the book of Hebrews were not equipped to feed themselves—to discern sacred or spiritual from profane or carnal. If you are in a dependent state, it is to your advantage to learn how you can wean yourself spiritually from the bottle. Some Christians over the years have lost their appetite for solid, spiritual food and need to be fed. Everyone should become less dependent on spiritual milk and instead become more capable of benefitting from solid food.

Day 11

GOD'S DISCIPLINE

Many times, if it hadn't been for the Lord disciplining us, we would continue down the wrong paths of life. Think about what happened to Jonah when he was disobedient to God, but God got him back on track as reluctant as he was to perform the task for which he was called. We are often like Jonah. We have our own agendas, but God in His love for us redirects us back to the right paths. Isn't God good that way? But, we often don't see discipline as an encouragement or a redirecting for our good. It is! When God disciplines it is to make us better people.

God's conviction of sin in our lives is an encouragement to grow. He redirects us when it comes to laying down our selfish pride and exchanges it for humility. God's discipline reflects His love relationship with us. God, as well as those of us humans who have people at heart, will never allow a person to go in the wrong direction without saying or doing something. Trust God just as you trusted your parents in their discipline to raise you up into quality individuals.

Hebrews 12:5-6
(5) And have you forgotten the encouraging words God spoke to you as his children? He said, "My child, don't make light of the Lord's discipline, and don't give up when he corrects you. (6) For the Lord disciplines those he loves, and he punishes each one he accepts as his child." (NLT)

Day 12

BE FAITHFUL TO YOUR CALL, MISSION, AND WITNESS

Many are called, but few are chosen. The call is not just for preachers or other church leaders, but to all believers. There are general calls, and there are special calls. The general calls are for all believers to fulfill the mandate of witness and to follow God. The special call is for those whom God has chosen for special assignments in the Body of Christ; we each have a special assignment. Some seem great and some seem small, but all are exclusive. Consult the Lord on what this is for you. Remain faithful in this work of Him who sent us while it is day, because the 'night' is coming when no man can work.

Jesus was faithful to His calling from God, even to giving up His life for the sins of the world. He calls you to be faithful to your calling; to take up your cross daily and follow in His footsteps as His disciple. And, He calls you to be His witness and to make disciples. With a heart shaped by grace, a mind shaped by His truth, a life shaped by His training, and a life shaped by adopting His ways, you show others what it means to live, love, and be an example for Jesus.

Matthew 28:18-20
> *(18) Then Jesus came to them and said, "All authority in heaven and on earth has been given to me. (19) Therefore go and make disciples of all nations, baptizing them in the name of the Father and of the Son and of the Holy Spirit, (20) and teaching them to obey everything I have commanded you. And surely I am with you always, to the very end of the age."*

Day 13

AN EXCEPTION TO THE POPULAR/COMMON RULE OF SOCIETY

Dare to be different. In this day when it seems like to some everything goes, do not be the same as the world. You are different! Don't try to imitate the world—the people of the world have their own agenda opposite of the people of God. Yours should be to live according to the Bible—the eternal Word of God.

While many in the church are diluting the Word in order to be "world friendly," and attempting to make the church look like the world, you are to be an exception to such rebellion and confusion. Align yourself as a true, genuine ambassador of God. The whole of scripture attests to the people of God as distinctive and uncommon to what was going on around them—to the sinful patterns and common rule of the day. Young and old in age should simply stand up for righteousness and truth.

God's way is the way to a civil, moral, decent, and good society where the people are striving to live a beautiful life as Christ would want. After all, He is our chief example—the Chief Cornerstone.

Day 14

BE THE BEST PERSON YOU CAN BE

Everyone was born with unique gifts inside of them. A common problem is that some want their gift and *someone else's also*. Why is that? It is often because that type of person wants all the glory that they can get all focused on them only. That is a selfish attitude and is against the principles of God. If people would accept their own unique gifting and not covet someone else's, then jealousy could subside.

As a result of this selfishness, a person can never be satisfied— restless, and always clamoring for more! The selfish and jealous person sees talents and gifts in others that they don't have and crave those things as well instead of developing their own unique gifts. The solution is to abide in your own calling, skills, and capabilities. You will find that you only have time to do what you are gifted to do and do those things well!

So spend your time developing your own God-given skills, abilities, and talents. No one can defeat you at being you. Indeed you can learn from others and incorporate those lessons into who you are. However, strive to be the best person you can be. Use your gifts and talents for the up-building of the Kingdom of God. Your gifts will edify the Body of Christ. The Spirit-filled believer is to "Speak to one another with psalms, hymns and spiritual songs." "Submit to one another out of reverence for Christ" (Eph 5:19, 21).

Day 15

A SNAPSHOT, OR PORTRAIT, OF THE GODLESS

Psalm 14:1-3
(1) The fool (morally deficient) says in his heart, "There is no God." They are corrupt, their deeds are vile; there is no one who does. (2) The Lord looks down from heaven on the sons of men to see if there are any who understand, any who seek God. (3) All have turned aside, they have together become corrupt; there is no one who does good, not even one.

Proverbs 14:12
"There is a way that seems right to a man, but in the end it leads to death."

These two passages speak to problems that are present in the world today where people are becoming more open to embracing things that are not of God. They have turned aside from God and become corrupt and vile. A large number of people are doing things their own way. Immorality is prevalent in society. People have become morally deficient and morally corrupt.

There needs to be a movement back to God and of seeking after His will for humanity. The key to a better world today is for people to commit to God and His church. There must be a resolve to uphold the will of God. God must be respected, honored, adored and extolled.

A snapshot or portrait of the godly is a man or woman who seeks God and seeks to do God's will.

Isaiah 55:6
'Seek the Lord while He may be found; call upon Him while He is near.'

Day 16

GOD'S TIME IS THE RIGHT TIME

Sometimes it appears that we've been waiting for a long time for an answer from the Lord or perhaps waiting on a blessing. Sometimes you may feel like they may never happen. Times like these often prompt the question, 'When will these come (through)?' Whatever you need the Lord to work out for you—just wait on Him! The scripture says (in Ecclesiastes), everything under the sun is in God's hands anyway and we don't have the controlling hand to do anything about it. All we need to do is relax and leave it to God after we have done our part in the matter. This is what the psalmist says to the Lord:

Psalm 31:15
My times are in your hands;
Deliver me from the hands of my enemies,
From those who pursue me.

Time is an interesting thing because we can't control it. And as humans, we don't like to wait on anything. Time is in the hands of God. It often seems like there is time for everything under the sun. At other times, it seems that things move just a little too slow. Then sometimes it appears time moves too fast! Things that we want to happen right now don't and things that want to slow down seem to speed up. Every month moves along so fast that before your eyes it's time to pay another month's worth of bills. The 'years of our lives' move by so fast and before you know it, lots of time has passed. Each day of the week moves by so fast, and for full-time workers, sometimes the

8-hour clock seems to slow down.

In reality, as David states, everything in our lives happen exactly at the right time, and it's God's timing (see 1 Samuel 19-24). At the time, David was trying to escape from King Saul who was out to destroy him. What you need for the Lord to move on your behalf—physical, emotional, financial, or spiritual—wait on the Lord. An old song says, 'He may not come when we want Him, but he's right on time.'

Day 17

OBSTACLES CAN BECOME OPPORTUNITIES

Opportunities to serve others are all around us. Christ wants His followers to be servants to those who are in need. Be an extension of Christ: His arms, hands, feet, heart, soul, and mind. Take every occasion to minister to people, just as Jesus would. Christ ministers through us! We can be a positive influence to others to bring about change. As followers of Christ, we can influence the lives of other encouraging them to stay in the race; to be positive in the midst of trying situations; to fight for life; to create relationships that will be a support system; and generally, to triumph. Jesus is always trying to get us to understand how He wants to use us.

Mark 6:51-52
(51) Then he climbed into the boat, and the wind stopped. They were totally amazed, (52) for they still didn't understand the significance of the miracle of the loaves. Their hearts were too hard

to take it in.

God became a human being in the person of Jesus and entered into covenant relationship with the people around Him. The Lord invested Himself into the lives of His disciples. He is our example of a genuine servant. Allow His Spirit to radiate through us to others. By this, help turn someone's obstacles around.

Jesus always finds ways to help us understand and deal with the problems of humanity and bring about transformation. How can you invest in the lives of people to make a difference? What will you do to allow God's love to influence the life of someone today?

Day 18

KOINONIA: THE BELOVED COMMUNITY OF BELIEVERS

In Greek, the members of the household of faith were known as the *koinonia*, which was the watchword of the early church in Acts. The beloved community encouraged one another in maintaining the life of salvation. Build one another up in the life of faith in Christ. The most valuable things are those things that money can't buy—the intangibles of inner-being—love, peace of mind, emotional and mental stability, a support system, and fellowship.

As Paul closes his letter to the Galatian church, he stresses the importance of helping one another stay on track spiritually. In doing so, he refers to the pride that edges God out and keeps us at arm's length from people.

Jesus didn't have this problem; on the contrary, He made it His mission to help those trapped in sin. When we develop an exalted sense of our own importance, pride cuts us off from humbly following Jesus' example. How does Jesus want you to follow in His footsteps of helping others today?

Galatians 6:3
If you think you are too important to help someone, you are only fooling yourself. You are not that important. (NLT)

Day 19

LOVING THE WORLD: THE SINFUL NATURE

1 John 2:15-16
(15) Do not love the world or anything in the world. If anyone loves the world, the love of the Father is not in him. (16) For everything in the world—the cravings of sinful man, the lust of his eyes and the boasting of what he has and does—comes not from the Father but from the world.

Rather than minding the things of the world, pay sincere attention to the things of God and it will pay off for you. Concerns put into proper perspective will certainly reap rewards. The sinful nature of man will most assuredly be counterproductive for you.

First John 2:15-16 warns us not to love the world (of Satan's creation) because it is a huge reservoir of influences to the budding kernel of pride in each of us. Pride causes selfish behaviors and attitudes. Selfishness thwarts the plans of Jesus for His people. Pride leads to other sins.

Spiritual victory is achieved when a person seeks after

God *first* and the Bible declares that all 'these things shall be added unto you': Our ambitions, hopes, and dreams for success will be achieved. We are not to seek after these things apart from God, without having God first in our lives is to be a servant of the world; we are more susceptible to doing whatever it takes to achieve these things, even if it means our downfall.

The Parable of the Pharisee and the Tax Collector provides an example, showing how destructive selfishness and pride can be to relationships: "The Pharisee stood and prayed thus with himself, 'God, I thank You that I am not like other men—extortioners, unjust, adulterers, or even as this tax collector. I fast twice a week; I give tithes of all that I possess'" (Lk 18:11-12). Pride can make a person become condescending and self-righteous, so that he sees himself as greater than others, which can lead to misusing them. Does that sound like the kind of person you want to be? Will you strive to mind the things of God without destroy pride today?

Day 20

THE GOLDEN GRAVEN IMAGE: ACTS OF IDOLATRY AND DISHONOR

One of the grossest acts of self-interest and lack of faith in God displayed in biblical history was when the children of Israel dishonored God by worshipping a golden calf (after being saved from attack by the Egyptians). Moses was taking too long for them, so Israel decided to take matters into their own hands—concocting a graven image to worship. What or who are you worshiping today?

Exodus 32:1-8

(1) When the people saw that Moses was so long in coming down from the mountain, they gathered around Aaron and said, "Come, make us gods who will go before us. As for this fellow Moses who brought us up out of Egypt, we don't know what has happened to him." (2) Aaron answered them, "Take off the gold earrings that your wives, your sons and your daughters are wearing, and bring them to me." (3) So all the people took off their earrings and brought them to Aaron. (4) He took what they handed him and made it into an idol cast in the shape of a calf, fashioning it with a tool. Then they said, "These are your gods, O Israel, who brought you up out of Egypt." (5) When Aaron saw this, he built an altar in front of the calf and announced, 'Tomorrow there will be a festival to the LORD." (6) So the next day the people rose early and sacrificed burnt offerings and presented fellowship offerings. Afterward they sat down to eat and drink and got up to indulge in revelry. (7) Then the LORD said to Moses, "Go down, because your people, whom you brought up out of Egypt, have become corrupt. (8) They have been quick to turn away from what I commanded them and have made themselves an idol cast in the shape of a calf. They have bowed down to it and sacrificed to it and have said, 'These are your gods, O Israel, who brought you up out of Egypt.'

Proverbs 14:12 says, "There is a way that seems right to a man, but its end is the way of death." Just as surely as the ancient Israelites blended paganism with worship of God, so do people today. In their ignorance and impatience, they did this in order to 'get things moving.' People today move in haste; they can't wait on God. Even though most of Israel wanted to worship the graven image, and a leader proclaimed it "a feast to the Lord," it did not make it so. Many times people do things in the name of the Lord, but God is not in it at all. Israel configured a nature of God according to their own desires. An example of this today would be to pervert the Word of God by manipulating what is written for your own benefit; that would also be a misrepresentation. Another example would be to simply make anything or anyone your god by idolizing it or them. It could even be family members. This is why Jesus Christ says (Matt 10:37-38, KJV), "He that loves father or mother more than me is not worthy of me: and he that loves son or daughter more than me is not worthy of me. And he that takes not his cross, and follows after me, is not worthy of me."

Day 21

JEHOVAH JIREH OUR PROVIDER: MIRACLES FOR OUR DAILY LIFE

Water, food, nature, life, and all things good, are all for the good of mankind. God makes the way for us to enjoy life. God is known biblically by several names, each giving a quality, function, or characteristic of Him. They give a picture of who God is and what He is about. Jehovah-Jireh is one of those signifying names of God as our Provider. This name was spoken by Abraham (Gen 22:14) as to the spot where Yahweh saw Abraham's need and provided a 'ram in the bush' for him—in the place of the near-sacrifice of his son—indicating that 'the Lord will provide.' He will provide for you too—a miracle every day.

The following passage shows how God provides for His people and also shows how people, including leaders, may err in receiving the blessings of Almighty God.

Numbers 20:8-13

(8) Take the staff, and you and your brother Aaron gather the assembly together. Speak to that rock before their eyes and it will pour out its water. You will bring water out of the rock for the community so they and their livestock can drink. (9) So Moses took the staff from the Lord's presence, just as he commanded him. (10) He and Aaron gathered the assembly together in front of the rock and Moses said to them, "Listen, you rebels, must we bring you water out of this rock?" (11) Then Moses raised his arm and struck the rock twice with his staff. Water gushed out, and the community and their livestock drank. (12) But the Lord said to Moses and Aaron, "Because you did not trust in me enough to honor me as holy in the sight of the Israelites, you will not bring this community into the land I give them." (13) These were the waters of Meribah,[a] where the Israelites quarreled with the Lord and where he was proved holy among them.

The above passage shows how God provided water for the people of Israel and their livestock. God gave Moses the instructions as to what to do. However, Moses committed a grave offense in that he: (1) Took credit to himself for what God had done for the people (verse 10); (2) disobeyed God by not talking to the rock (verse 11); (3) lost his temper (struck the rock twice when told to speak to it; verse 11); (4) used a harsh expression addressing the people (called them rebels; verse 10); (5) was provoked about their need and resented them (verse 10); (6) was guilty of unbelief, because he did not trust the power of God like God needed his help (verse 12); (7) failed to glorify God before His people (verse 12); and lastly, (8) rebelled against God (verse 24). Moses' brother Aaron suffered the same punishment as Moses because he was with him in this offense. God did perform the miracle for the people, even though Moses acted in a way that displeased God.

Many of us act in this manner by not trusting God or not obeying His commands to us. The fact is that many times God will still provide for us; but, we must not make a practice of disobeying, disrespecting, or dishonoring Him (acting as if someone else performed miracles for us). It is God who provides life and sustenance for us each day. The point is that God *will* provide your needs on a daily basis, regardless of how difficult it may be. The provisions of God are sure and sufficient every morning. Trust in God because He will provide for you.

Day 22

WHERE IS THE JOY?

Psalm 28:7
> *The Lord is my strength and my shield;*
> *My heart trusts in him, and he helps me.*
> *My heart leaps for joy,*
> *And with my song I praise him.*

The great irony of our generation is that never before has humanity experienced so much material affluence, yet at the same time, so much sorrow and depression. Joy is a word that many lives do not know. But God wants us to be filled with joy. Psalm 100:2 tells us to "Worship the Lord with gladness; come before him with joyful songs." How can we get joy back into our lives and a song into our hearts? God is our song! God is our joy! God is our strength!

In Psalm 28, King David wrote, "The Lord is my strength and my shield; my heart trusts in him, and he helps me. My heart leaps for joy, and with my song I praise him." We could look at this verse and see two distinct ideas. The first is that God was David's savior, and the second is that David was a joyful and grateful person. Hence, we must make God our savior; and we must joyful and grateful for God's deliverance. Do not miss the substance of the verse's message. It contains one connected thought: David saw God as the source of his strength, and therefore he had joy and a song in his heart. Joy is found in Christ! He is our joy, peace, hope, strength and shield! The joy of the Lord is our strength! Be encouraged and joyful!

Day 23

THE STANDARD

As a child of the King, we should look like Him— meaning we should love like Christ, we should live like Christ, and we should have compassion like Christ. He expects us to live up to His standards. The standard is we must strive to be like Jesus Christ!

The theme of the book of Ephesians is the church and Christ's Body. It gives the foundation for all believers as a part of Christ's Body. We belong to Christ! He is our example! We are heirs and joint heirs of the King!

Ephesians 1:3-7

> *(3) Praise be to the God and Father of our Lord Jesus Christ, who has blessed us in the heavenly realms with every spiritual blessing in Christ. (4) For he chose us in him before the creation of the world to be holy and blameless in his sight. In love (5) he predestined us to be adopted as his sons through Jesus Christ, in accordance with his pleasure and will—(6) to the praise of his glorious grace, which he has freely given us in the One (Christ) he loves. (7) In him we have redemption through his blood, the forgiveness of sins, in accordance with the riches of God's grace.*

Day 24

GOD'S GRACE

Is it hard for you when God shows grace and mercy to your enemies? Those who have hurt you? The reality is that God's way is to treat everyone the same and grant mercy to whomever needs it. Jonah got upset when God showed favor to his enemies and ordered him to deliver the word. Man, was that hard for Jonah, and such a situation may also be hard for you sometimes as well. You may not understand it, but Christ shows mercy to all. That's a portrait of Christ, and as *His* portrait you are expected to do the same. Love your enemies. Love those who persecute you. Love those who say all manner of evil things against us. Love and show respect to everyone.

Like Jonah, we gratefully receive God's grace for ourselves. But the test of our hearts comes when God shows grace to people who have been our antagonists. Do you respond with the same joy when others receive His

forgiveness and grace? God's compassion and love knows
no bounds. Pray to the Lord for love and compassion.
Jonah prayed to the Lord:

Jonah 4:2-3
> *Isn't this what I said, Lord, when I was still at home? That is*
> *what I tried to forestall by fleeing to Tarshish. I knew that you*
> *are a gracious and compassionate God, slow to anger and*
> *abounding in love, a God who relents from sending calamity.*
> *Now, Lord, take away my life, for it is better for me to die than*
> *to live.*

Amen!

Day 25

RESPECT AND HONOR GOD NO MATTER WHAT

To live as if there is no God is form of disrespect and
dishonor to Him. It is possible curse God by your
language and actions. Have you ever said or done harsh
things directed at God? Violated His Word? Or dismissed
God entirely? For example, some may accuse God when
He doesn't act or (re)act to our selfish claims and needs.
Just because Christ doesn't come when we want Him to
doesn't mean that He doesn't love us or care about us.
People also think that this life in Christ is futile and hard to
live. Remember that His Spirit is forever with us to help
us to live this life, if we honor and respect Him.

Sometimes we look at the arrogant and people of the
world as supremely blessed while walking around as

mourners, pouting and feeling unblessed because of our negative situations. We lose faith in Jesus Christ! It may seem that those 'of the world' are being blessed when our lives are at stake. Many times we become lackadaisical in worship and feeling harsh against the Lord because our lives are not as we desire. We should respect God no matter what!

Jeremiah complained to the Lord in chapter 12 about how the wicked prospered (vv. 1-3):

(1) You are always righteous, Lord,
when I bring a case before you.
Yet I would speak with you about your justice:
Why does the way of the wicked prosper?
Why do all the faithless live at ease?
(2) You have planted them, and they have taken root;
they grow and bear fruit.
You are always on their lips
but far from their hearts.
(3) Yet you know me, Lord;
You see me and test my thoughts about you.

People who are experiencing difficult times often cry out, "Why, God?" "Why are You allowing this to happen?" "Why *me*?" or "When are You going to intervene?" Even if God doesn't come when we think He should, we must still trust in God! Jeremiah had grown weary of the evil going on around him. The Lord later answered Jeremiah, assuring him that there will be justice upon the nations.

Malachi wrote in Judea between the time of return from Babylon and Christ's birth. During that period God's people had grown lackadaisical in their worship, yet a faithful few remained:

Malachi 3:13-16
*(13) "You have said harsh things against me," says the Lord.
"Yet you ask, 'What have we said against you?' (14) "You have
said, 'It is futile to serve God. What did we gain by carrying out
his requirements and going about like mourners before the Lord
Almighty? (15) But now we call the arrogant blessed. Certainly
the evildoers prosper, and even those who challenge God escape.'"
(16) Then those who feared the Lord talked with each other, and
the Lord listened and heard. A scroll of remembrance was written
in his presence concerning those who feared the Lord and honored
his name.*

God honored those who honored Him and said in
verse 17, 'they shall be mine.' The people who dishonored
God blamed Him for their plight. It is true, they were
experiencing difficult times, just as many of us in this day
in time experience difficulties, but we still respect and
honor to God 'no matter what.'

Day 26

ON TRUSTING JESUS CHRIST AND OTHERS

Matthew 17:19
*Then the disciples came to Jesus in private and asked, "Why
couldn't we drive it out?"*

To ask another person for help means that you have
developed a relationship where there is mutual trust,
whether it is a friend or a family member. One does not
entrust their life, thoughts, and secrets with just anyone—

it has to be a person of trust. We all need someone we can trust in order to share and talk to. Certain people are put into our lives to share on the human level, to be a support system.

In this kind of relationship, there is a deep trust where you believe that the person will be sensitive and caring to your needs. Do you have such a person in your life? Is there someone who you can really trust with your deepest secrets? Do you have someone who you can share your deepest struggles? It is a special blessing to have someone to talk to, like a spouse, a friend, and a confidante. There are people who also pay a lot of money to talk to a counselor, adviser, or psychiatrist.

But, it is even better to know and trust Jesus Christ. You have to know him, love Him, and trust Him in order for Him to work for you! Trust is the outcome of transformed personal relationships. When you have been transformed—saved—you can't help but trust Christ for all of your needs! Just like when we serve other people with humility and integrity, a relationship and a bond develops that causes that person to trust you. They believe that you are on their side and want the best for them. They believe you have their best interests at heart. Trust is often built slowly, over a long period of time. It is broken easily when we attack or misuse a person instead of helping them defeat their challenges. How can you develop your trust in the Lord? How can you build trust with others today? The disciples trusted Jesus. They talked to Him, asked Him questions, communed with Him, and prayed with Him. Trust Him!

Day 27

HOPE AGAIN! DON'T GIVE UP!

When it appears all hope is gone, that is the time to hold your head up, give it all to the Lord, and hope again. Jesus Christ is your Savior for the total man—mind, heart, soul, spirit, and body. When you lose hope, life is not worth living, but when you regain the will to live life more abundantly.

Psalm 27:14
> *Wait for the Lord;*
> *Be strong and take heart*
> *And wait for the Lord.*

That is it in a nutshell. That is all it takes—a change of heart and mind—as the scripture says, 'wait for the Lord; be strong and take heart.' Have faith!

Hope is a word that we toss around a lot, but I'm not sure that we always fully understand its meaning. It isn't until we've lived hope—until we have been in a dark place where we needed to find the light of hope—that we can really know what the word means. After a bad situation, there's the hope of having faith that things will be all right. And there's also the hope gained after a challenge when things turn out differently than initially hoped—the hope we previously had is strengthened. Hoping again is like being born again. All things become new! Brand new!

Day 28

IN REMEMBRANCE OF CHRIST

Humble yourself at the feet of Christ. Honor God in all things, because He honored us by giving His Son and His Son gave His life for our sins. Always remember Christ and the love He showed towards us. I appreciate what Christ did! Do you?

1 Corinthians 11:28-29
> *(28) A man ought to examine himself before he eats of the bread and drinks of the cup. (29) For anyone who eats and drinks without recognizing the body of the Lord eats and drinks judgment on himself.*

Partaking of the sacraments was a form of remembrance and worship of Jesus.' Grasping the impact of not only Christ's sacrifice, but also of who He is, determines our (level of) observance or of our worship. To prevent taking the bread and the cup in a careless and unappreciative manner, Paul charges us to examine ourselves, discerning the Lord's body. "Examine" means to test, prove, or scrutinize to determine whether a thing is genuine. "Discern" means to separate, discriminate, or to make a distinction for the purpose of giving preference. I urge you to remember the supreme sacrifice that Jesus offered for you through worship and in testifying of Him.

Day 29

ON SEEKING GOD DAILY

God delights to find you earnestly seeking His wisdom, to see your face turned toward Him in expectation and confidence. Your problems don't outpace the Lord God's wisdom or His Spirit's ability to lead you. He waits for you to turn to Him. Whatever today holds for you, He invites you to seek Him, to experience His presence, and to depend on His wisdom. Will He find you looking up to Him today?

Psalm 14:2
> *The Lord looks down from heaven on all mankind to see if there is any who understand, any who seek God.*

It is good wisdom to seek God for all of our needs on a daily basis and most of all to thank Him for what He has already done. We need God in our lives! Since we do not know what the future holds for us, we need His infinite wisdom and knowledge operating in our lives, because God is all-knowing. The hymn writer Ira F. Stanphill says,

> *I don't know about tomorrow, I just live from day to day. I don't borrow from its sunshine, for its skies may turn to gray. I don't worry o'er the future, for I know what Jesus said; and today I'll walk beside Him, for He knows what is ahead. Many things about tomorrow I don't seem to understand; but I know who holds tomorrow, and I know who holds my hand.*

Yes, it is Jesus!

We make our plans. We mark dates and appointments

in our date books. We plan our budgets. Preachers and teachers plan messages and lessons plans. People who travel as entertainers, sports figures, speakers, etc. all plan tours and dates. Day to day, we plan what to eat, where to go, and what to do, but the truth is, we don't know how our days will really turn out. One thing we do know is that God is in control of times and seasons and of the past, the present, and the future. Continue to put your trust completely in God.

Day 30

MATURE CHRISTIANS

Ephesians 4:14
Then we will no longer be infants, tossed back and forth by the waves, and blown here and there by every wind of teaching and by the cunning and craftiness of men in their deceitful scheming.

A mature Christian is not necessarily determined by the age of the person, but rather by his or her growth and development in the Word and the way of the Lord! A mature Christian is one who will not be swayed by any and every doctrine proclaimed by men, but will stay true to the Word of God. A mature Christian will not be buffeted by any or anything that comes his or her way, but will be strong in faith. Satan's craftiness will not deter the thinking and heart of a mature believer.

A mature Christian is one who will not fall for the sinful and diabolical schemes that Satan and his imps push. A mature Christian 'shall not be moved'! A mature Christian stands on the Word of God. It's that simple...

It is common for people to take the easy way, the path of least resistance. They allow themselves to be blown along with the prevailing cultural wind, whether in fashion, sports, art, music, politics, or sadly, ethics and morals. The God's will is of foremost importance to the true believer. Mature Christians take no thought of the course or direction that the world takes; no matter what news relays to them, or dictates. They do not follow along with the current trends just because it is easier to "go with the flow." Don't be ruled by the "majority," but instead esteem the "few" who travel the road of holiness. Don't count your mistakes or circumstances; however, own that things sometimes occur because a person may not have been on the Lord's straight path. The mature Christian—child of God—honors God's morality and precepts, applying them to life.

Day 31

DO NOT REMAIN A BABE IN CHRIST FOREVER

Our spiritual growth and development is important to our Lord and should be important to us as well. There is nothing worse than a Christian who has supposedly been saved for a while and has not grown. Christ expects us to mature in the Word enough to live out our salvation with fear (awe) and trembling (respect) for the Lord. For instance, you should be able to distinguish good from evil and not confuse the two.

Babies have to drink milk until they have sufficiently matured enough to eat a regular diet. Christians should not always need to be babied and fed milk forever—there comes a time when a Christian should be able to eat a hearty meal!

Hebrews 5:13-14
> *(13) Anyone who lives on milk, being still an infant, is not acquainted with the teaching about righteousness. (14) But solid food is for the mature, who by constant use have trained themselves to distinguish good from evil.*

The Hebrews had to be reminded in the strongest of terms that the just shall live by faith, and that God was not pleased with those who turned and ran in the day of battle. We do not want to allow ourselves to get in that fix. Nor do we want to become discouraged, thinking we will never measure up to what God requires of us or, "This task is too hard." Do not become overwhelmed either with living the life of Christ. With His help, we can do it. The Holy Spirit strengthens us! Maturing in Christ strengthens us to do His work.

Jesus, indeed, warned that the way is narrow and difficult, but it is not impossible because God has promised to never give us something that is too difficult for us to bear. God plays the game, as it were, according to the abilities of each individual. Though there is a standard against which everyone is judged, everyone is judged fairly—according to their natural ability and according to the gifts that God has given to them. Also, "to whom much is given, from him much will be required" (Lk 12:48).

Day 32

PROPHETIC WARNING: THE DAY OF THE LORD IS NEAR AS IN NOAH'S DAY (BE READY WHEN HE COMES!)

Christ will definitively establish His rule upon the earth. As is the days of Noah, people should not ignore the signs, but should pay attention to what is coming down the pike.

Revelation 6:15
Then the kings of the earth, the princes, the generals, the rich, the mighty, and every slave and every free man hid in caves and among the rocks of the mountains.

"Every slave and every free man" refers to the scope of God's judgment. It extends universally to various classes of people. Armed with far more knowledge about God and His plan than their masters, God's people will be able to put the horrifying events into perspective for the already-humbled cave-dwellers. As the Day of the Lord nears:

1. Assure others that Christ will soon end the maddening chaos by establishing His rule on earth.
2. Tell them the living can expect to see His return ("every eye will see Him"; Rev 1:7).
3. Inform them that, at His return, they can expect to see God's people rising in the air to meet Him (I Thess 4:17).
4. Instruct them that, once Christ consolidates His rule, the terror will subside, as the healing waters from His

throne take their effect (Ezek 47:1-12; Rev 22:1-2).

5. Enjoin them to make their way to Jerusalem when conditions begin to settle down, where they will be taught by Christ, the Lamb of God.

Since every eye will see Christ return (Rev 1:7), we can deduce that the rigors of the Day of the Lord will open the caves.

In Noah's day, there was partying, ignoring God, and immorality abounding, as so it is now. Further, some do not believe that there is a hell or that the devil exists. Demonic influences are happening all around us and many of us do not see it. The devil is working his plots, schemes, and plans and is using many people to help him—even in the church world. Open your eyes and beware of the demonic forces surrounding you. There is a real devil plotting all the time to take your attention away from the things of God. Before you know it, Satan would have wreaked havoc on you. 'Be aware Satan is up and down the earth seeking whom he may devour.' Sneak attacks are his method of operation. Be alert! Your redemption draws nigh!

Day 33

THERE IS HOPE FOR THE FUTURE

No matter how dark it is, I encouraged you to stay positive and look to the Lord above. Jesus is the Light of the World! He is our hope! He is our strength! In Christ, there is no darkness! Only light! He is our hope for the future!

Numbers 15:18–20
(18) "Speak to the Israelites and say to them: 'When you enter the land to which I am taking you (19) and you eat the food of the land, present a portion as an offering to the LORD. (20) Present a loaf from the first of your ground meal and present it as an offering from the threshing floor.'"

The hope for the future is in giving of ourselves and of our resources to help one another wherever we can. Our text lifts that very point for us not to forget to 'present a portion of what we have as an offering to the Lord.' Don't be selfish, but share the light of life with others and you will be giving to God.

Despair flooded the Israelites' camp all that night. The people cried about their present circumstance, their future, and they even longed for their past that included slavery, hardship, and suffering. They lost hope and faith that night and defiantly turned away from God.

God was angered by His people's lack of faith. Hadn't He taken them out of Egypt and sustained them in the desert? Could He not have brought them into the land that He had promised them as well? As a result of their doubt, God punished the people and promised that they would not enter the land. Instead, they would wander in the desert for 40 years where they would learn the kind of faith needed to enter the Holy Land. The light of life comes through faith, trust, believing, and sharing the substance of God. Many times individuals suffer great sorrow and pain because they do not look to God for their present and future sustenance.

Your hope for the future lies in your faith in the Lord and Savior, Jesus Christ. Your hope for the future and for the present is in *knowing* Jesus Christ and trusting in Him. Philippians 4:4-7 gives us the way to find joy and hope now and always:

Philippians 4:4-7
> *(4) Rejoice in the Lord always. I will say it again: Rejoice! (5) Let your gentleness be evident to all. The Lord is near. (6) Do not be anxious for anything, but in everything, by prayer and petition, with thanksgiving, present your requests to God. (7) And the peace of God, which transcends all understanding, will guard your hearts and your minds in Jesus Christ.*

Day 34

THE SALT OF THE EARTH AND THE LIGHT OF THE WORLD

God-Given Influence

Believer, you can help to shape the world around you. You should be the positive influence in your surroundings. You have been created in the image and likeness of God, which is a position of honor. Therefore, God expects you to walk in that honor and shine brightly to the world around you.

Jesus gave us a mandate in Matthew 28:19ff to 'make disciples of every one we come in contact with,' not only by what you say, but how you live your life. Let someone see Jesus in you. It is through the Holy Spirit that we gain the power and strength to be that positive influence. How will you influence the lives of people today and show them the way to Jesus Christ? How will you exalt God in your lifestyle? Can people see Jesus in you? Direct someone to Christ today!

In the first chapter of John, Andrew, Simon Peter's brother, was one of the two who heard what John had said and who had followed Jesus. The first thing Andrew did was to find his brother Simon and tell him, "We have found the Messiah" (that is, the Christ). And he brought him to Jesus (John 1:40-42). This verse lets us know that Jesus' disciples used their new found faith to influence others to come to Christ, including their own family members. It is imperative that you help guide family and friends toward Jesus. That is the greatest witness of all!

When God gives you His Spirit, He gives you the courage to witness to others. The similitude on salt and light in Matthew 5:13-16 cites the words of Jesus as He describes how followers of Christ should be seen in the world. Jesus describes it in terms of salt and light.

> *(13) "You are the salt of the earth. But if the salt loses its saltiness, how can it be made salty again? It is no longer good for anything, except to be thrown out and trampled by men. (14) "You are the light of the world. A city on a hill cannot be hidden. (15) Neither do people light a candle and put it under a bowl. Instead they put it on its stand, and it gives light to everyone in the house. (16) In the same way, let your light shine before men, that they may see your good deeds and praise your Father in heaven.*

Let your light shine! You are a witness for the Lord in the world!

Day 35

THE REAL TEMPLE OF GOD

Do you find yourself worthy to be a "living sanctuary"?
God wants to dwell within each of us. You and I are the
real temples of God—the real church.

1 Corinthians 3:16-17
*(16) Don't you know that you yourselves are God's temple and
that God's Spirit lives in you? (17) If anyone destroys God's
temple, God will destroy him; for God's temple is sacred, and you
are that temple.*

One aspect of this responsibility to the body is, of
course, caring for our physical bodies. Because we belong
to God, we are holy and are integral parts of the body of
Christ. Responsibility weighs upon us with greater
intensity than those who are not a part of the Body of
Christ. In John 14:23, Jesus illustrates the closeness of our
relationship with God, saying, "If anyone loves Me, he will
obey My teaching. My Father will love him, and We will
come to him and make Our home with him."

Under the old covenant, God is mysterious, dwelled in
the temple, and revealed Himself in various ways—as a
pillar of fire, pillar of cloud, His voice as a sound of
rushing water, and as a burning bush, etc. Under the *new*
covenant, we *become the temple of God,* and God becomes
more personal with us.

In I Corinthians 6:15-20, Paul clearly confirms the
concept that we are the living sanctuaries of God:

(15) Do you not know that your bodies are members of Christ

himself? Shall I then take the members of Christ and unite them with a prostitute? Never! (16) Do you not know that he who unites himself with a prostitute is one with her in body? For it is said "The two will become one flesh." (17) But he who unites himself with the Lord is one with Him in Spirit. (And because you are God's Temple you are to) (18) Flee from sexual immorality. All other sins a man commits are outside his body, but he who sins sexually sins against his own body. (19) Do you not know that your body is the temple of the Holy Spirit, who is in you, whom you have received from God? You are not your own; (20) You were bought at a price. Therefore honor God with your body.

Day 36

COURAGE REQUIRES FAITH

Courage has many faces. Sometimes courage and bravery looks like fearlessness; sometimes it looks like waiting patiently; sometimes it is reflected in humble obedience. Jesus courageously faced the cross; Mary courageously watched her Son suffer; the women courageously went to anoint His body. Always God-honoring courage is motivated by love and requires faith. How is God calling you to live bravely and courageously today?

It is not always easy to stand for God in this present age; it is particularly challenging because even in the church there are people who will challenge and combat sound doctrine. On every side there may be a test of your faith. The psalmist, King David writes:

Psalm 27:14
Wait patiently for the Lord. Be brave and courageous. Yes, wait patiently for the Lord. (NLT)

God is pleased with every follower of Christ when we wait on Him. Here is a formula for success in any area of life: Faith + Belief + Trust = Courage + Confidence + Bravery. Consider this passage:

Proverbs 3:5-6
(5) 'Trust the Lord with all your heart and lean not on your own understanding; (6) in all your ways acknowledge Him, and He will direct your paths (make your paths straight).'

Day 37

WHO'S ON THE LORD'S SIDE?

This question poses a challenge to the Body of Christ: If you testify to being a follower of Jesus Christ, then does your life truly exemplify that you are you on the Lord's side?

Numbers 14:41–42
But Moses said, "Why are you disobeying the Lord's command? This will not succeed! Do not go up, because the Lord is not with you. You will be defeated by your enemies."

Those who are on the Lord's side must not disobey Lord God's commands. Whatever the Lord says, do it! What He says not to do, don't do it! This will ensure either your victory or your defeat! Thus says the Lord!

Abraham Lincoln once said: "Sir, my concern is not

whether God is on our side; my greatest concern is to be on God's side, for God is always right." The President made a very remarkable, wise, and logical statement—and full of truth. God is always right!

When you obey God, there is no worry about the outcome of any situation. You will reach your promised land when you follow the directions, instructions, precepts, and principles of God. You won't have to worry about "Red Seas," "lands filled with giants," or any problem or negative situation. What a privilege it is to carry everything to God in prayer and obey the Lord's commands—stay on the Lord's side.

If God doesn't approve of where you are in your life—your lifestyle, plans, agendas, passions, then there will be a great barrier between you and victory. In a sense, David says it all in Psalm 127:1:

"...Unless the Lord builds the house, its builders labor in vain. Unless the Lord watches over us (the city), the watchmen stand guard in vain."

All is vain if we fail to follow the precepts of the Lord. Obeying God and staying in line with His will is foundational to being on the Lord's side. Whose side are you on? I'm on the Lord's side!

Day 38

PERSEVERANCE THROUGH TRIALS

James 1:12
> *Blessed is the man who perseveres under trial, because when he has stood the test, he will receive the crown of life, that God has promised to those who love him.*

The above verse gives an overview of what James' message was to his people. He ministered to the people during the dispersion of the Hebrew nation and all of the followers of Christ due to persecution and trial because of their faith in Jesus Christ. Generally, the theme of his book deals with Christian living in the midst of trials. He was a pastor to the people, encouraging them to persevere. He exhorted them (in James 1:2-4) to:

> *(2) Consider it pure joy, my brothers, whenever you face trials of many kinds, (3) because you know that the testing of your faith produces perseverance. (4) Let perseverance finish its work so that you may be mature and complete, not lacking anything.*

This passage tells us that when all of the trials and suffering are over, the result is pure victory and eternal reward of the 'crown of life.' Therefore, the testing of our faith brings blessings to the steadfast. There are blessings for the followers of Christ in this present life and in the life to come.

"Hardships often prepare ordinary people for an extraordinary destiny"—C.S. Lewis

Have you experienced this? When you have gone through suffering and pain, the outcome is usually a sense of peace and joy. I have personally said, 'That wasn't as bad as I thought it would be.' We must persevere in this life to achieve success and reward. Many persons who have reached success in life have this testimony of having started out in a bad place. Please remember that trouble doesn't last always.

Day 39

STOP RUNNING FROM GOD

There are a few people in this category of 'running from God': 1) People who are already professing Christians, but who are not honoring their call from the Lord, 2) Those who aren't professing Christians and won't seek the Lord, and 3) There are some who are working in an area of which God did not call them. In either case, there is a need for obedience to the call of the Lord. Do what God has inspired you to do.

We all know the story of Jonah, God's reluctant and rebellious prophet. His attempt to run from God's call ended in failure and increasingly disastrous situations. At the end of his rope, he called out to God, who had been waiting for Jonah's change of heart. All along, God had been orchestrating events so that Jonah would finally cry out to Him instead of running from Him. Where do you need to call out to God? He waits, ready to answer.

God is calling everyone to or for something. Listen for the voice of God—sometimes it's a still small voice. The important thing is to hear the call, move to perform it, God will be glorified, and you will be blessed.

Jonah 2:1-2
(1) From inside the fish Jonah prayed to the Lord his God. (2) He said: "In my distress I called to the Lord, and he answered me. From deep in the realm of the dead I called for help, and you listened to my cry."

It is not possible to run from God anyway because He is everywhere at the same time (omnipresent). In our flesh, we often are moved to follow our own desires instead of God's. As followers of Christ, we should aim to always please the Lord. Always resolve to do the will of God. Do not run from what God wants for you; it is always for your good.

Day 40

YOUR TEARS

Jesus Wept—John 11:35 (see also Eccl 3:1-8)

John 11:35 is determined to be the shortest verse in the Bible. It shows Jesus in His humanity as he wept for Mary and Martha as they lamented the death of their brother Lazarus. This narrative shows that Jesus loved this family as all families and He was saddened by their sadness. Even though He knew that Lazarus would be raised from the dead by His supernatural power, He yet showed an aspect of His humanity. Jesus Christ displayed the human emotion of shedding tears. The preacher in Ecclesiastes noted that 'there is a time to cry and a time to cease from crying.'

Your tears touch the heart of God. They may be temporary relief from deep pain and hurt. Tears may be of sadness *or* of joy! Society teaches that it is a sign of weakness to cry, especially for a man. But, crying is a coping mechanism from God to cleanse the inward parts of a human. It brings your soul to a place of stability until complete relief comes. Know that God is your peace, serenity, stability, comfort, hope, and the source of wholeness. Tears cleanse the soul and bring healing and wholeness to our hearts and minds.

Tears in the spiritual sense show humility, brokenness, conviction, compassion, devotion, adoration, and love to the object of our affection. Some tears on the negative end may indicate anger or frustration. On a personal note, I am blessed and my heart is "strangely warmed" when in the presence of God—in praise, worship, or study of the Word of God—whether in fellowship with the Body of Christ or at home, either place brings tears of joy as I worship the Lord in the beauty of holiness. To feel the presence of God is to meet Him at the altar of the heart. To call on the Lord and He touches us is a marvelous and glorious experience. New every morning! No wonder the songwriter said, "I'm Glad to Be in the Number One More Time."

The Holy Spirit penetrates the heart and touches the spirit of a person, ministering to us. The Lord touches my heart, my mind, and my soul. That's why I love preaching and teaching the Word, because I can pour into the lives of others, but first the Word speaks to me!

There is something about the Spirit of God that brings harmony to the broken pieces of the inwards parts of man and says to go on in the name of Jesus. His Spirit brings us into unity as we live in these carnal frames. Get in touch with God through His Spirit. I love to worship God! Can I get a witness?

Day 41

THE MINISTRY OF COMPASSION

People with needs surrounded Jesus. They came to be healed, to hear Him teach, to be fed, to be amazed. Jesus wasn't oblivious to their presence or His opportunities to impact them; He often met their needs, but He wasn't enslaved to them. Jesus expects us to minister to the needs of people also. We need to discern which needs people have and determine how to meet their needs. Just like Jesus we must carry out the needs of God's people according to God's vision and goals so that we all can live like He desires for us to—we help one another.

Mark 3:7-8
(7) Jesus went out to the lake with his disciples, and a large crowd followed him. (8) They came from all over Galilee, Judea, Jerusalem, Idumea, from east of the Jordan River, and even from as far north as Tyre and Sidon. The news about his miracles had spread far and wide, and vast numbers of people came to see him.

We must be compassionate to one another in order to try to reach them for Christ. When we reach out to people, we become an ambassador of Jesus Christ. The love of Christ dwells within us richly and spreads abroad to whomever we reach. Because we love the Lord, we love people also and minister to them with our gifts, talents, and skills—out of heartfelt compassion. When we fulfill the ministry of compassion, the Body of Christ will grow and prosper. God has called us to selflessness. That is real love!

Day 42

THE GREAT COMMISSION: JESUS SENT US

The Great Commission is found in different forms in the four gospels. In Matthew 28:18-20 Jesus says,

(18) "All authority in heaven and on earth has been given to me. (19) Therefore go and make disciples of all nations, baptizing them in the name of the Father and of the Son and of the Holy Spirit, (20) and teaching them to obey everything I have commanded you. And surely I am with you always, to the very end of the age."

Jesus commissioned you to be a witness of Him. Christians are called upon by Jesus Christ to be witnesses of Him wherever we find ourselves in all areas of life. Some are called for special missions and all of us are chosen to be general witnesses for Jesus. Your life is to be lived with a definite purpose. You are not saved to do nothing, but just as God sent His Son into the world, then Jesus in turn sends you. This is your purpose!

The gospel accounts of Jesus' life reflect a life lived on purpose. Wherever He went, whatever He did, nothing kept Him from fulfilling God's purposes in each setting. He focused on God's vision for the world and God's purpose for His life. As painful as He knew the Cross would be for Him, Jesus fulfilled that mission. Just as God sent Jesus, Jesus sends His disciples. He sends us in the power of the Holy Spirit to reveal the Father's love and salvation wherever we go. Where is He sending you today?

John 17:18
"As you sent me into the world, I have sent them into the world."

You are to be on a mission to use your abilities to touch the lives of people within your sphere of influence. Jesus equips you by the indwelling of the Holy Spirit. As you go about your daily life, share with people in a myriad of ways: a smile, a helping hand, an example of a life that shows the Christ within us. Live life on purpose—on a daily mission for the Savior.

Day 43

MISDIAGNOSED PROBLEMS FROM THE INNER MAN

Hannah (1 Samuel 1:1ff), was misdiagnosed by her husband—her priest. She suffered from internal hurt, pain, disappointment, and was the object of ridicule (by her husband's other wife who had 10 children). The outward expression of her pain is not what her husband Elkanah suspected. Hannah had to share with her priest that she was not drunk as he supposed, but that she had an unanswered request to God to have a son for her husband. Most of the problems of people, saint or sinner, stems from the inward parts of a person. Only Jesus Christ can minister to the needs of the inner person by His Spirit.

People often have internal problems that do not necessarily show on the outside. Truth of the matter is that most people try to hide their feelings from family, friends, and from their pastors. Psychiatrists usually ask individuals, 'now, what seems to be bothering you?' What problems are you facing today?

Most of the time, there is a need for you to share what is bothering you so that the proper help can be rendered. If you are suffering from problems, hurt, and pain, find someone to share it with so that you may receive help. Ultimately, it is God through Jesus Christ, executed by the Holy Spirit, who will give the help that you really need. Be honest with God and yourself about concerns that you may have. You should also have someone you can trust with your feelings and emotions to be able to talk with.

Unfulfilled longings from the inner person can lead to depression, frustration, anguish, suicide, or hurting other people. These undiagnosed problems from our 'inner man' must be addressed. Allow Jesus to help you through His Spirit and through others for whom the Lord has gifted.

Day 44

VICTORY

Psalm 33:21
   In Him our hearts rejoice, for we trust in his holy name.

On the Holy Spirit: Riding the Wings of the Wind

I view our very existence on the fact that the Holy Spirit is in the atmosphere. The Holy Spirit is always with us, directing and guiding us. I view it as though the Holy Spirit rides on the wings of the wind. The Bible even describes the Holy Spirit as a 'rushing mighty wind' on the Day of Pentecost. The analogy of the wind is used in several instances to denote how the Spirit can blow and move as the wind and travel from place to place, heart to heart, performing His task in the world. Jesus even told Nicodemus in John 3:8ff, in reference to the Holy Spirit, that the:

   'Wind blows wherever it pleases. You hear the sound, but you cannot tell where it comes from or where it is going.'

With this knowledge, you should always feel confident that in the Lord you can and will have victory in any circumstance. That should be reassuring! He is available to bring joy to your heart, peace to your confusion, and hope to your negative situations. This can happen for you by simply trusting in God and His Son, Jesus Christ.

A sad but true reality is that nothing threatens a person's bond with God more than going through hard times. The number one reason that people leave the faith is because they have gone through tragedy. They are left bitter, disillusioned, and with deep sadness.

The Other Side of Difficulty

The other side of difficulty is *victory!* The same problems that can drive you from God are the very things that can lead you right (back) to God. Riding on the wings of the Holy Spirit of God to receive the blessings of the Lord! Difficulties make are to make you better. They make us stronger—if we allow God's help. You can't allow our difficulties to cause our destruction or death. Rather, you must trust in His holy name. Through the Father, Son, and the Holy Spirit, you have victory! You are truly blessed! Victory is yours!

Day 45

CONQUER THOSE OBSTACLES AND MOUNTAINS

Deuteronomy 1:6–7
(6) The Lord our God said to us at Horeb, "You have stayed long enough at this mountain. (7) Break camp and advance into the hill country of the Amorites; go to all the nighboring peoples in the Arabah, in the mountains, in the western foothills, in the Negev and along the coast, to the land of the Canaanites and to Lebanon, as far as the great river, the Euphrates."

"You Have Stayed Long Enough"

The passage above gives a command by God to conquer their mountains because they have stayed there in the same spot long enough. It was time to move forward to receive their blessings that the Lord had already promised to them.

Do you find yourself in the same rut you've been in for quite some time? This account should give us all the incentive to make some changes in our lives to conquer those things that have been left undone too long. God is saying to us: 'You have stayed long enough!' It is time to overcome your mountains.

Around 520 BCE Zerubbabel was charged with a momentous task. He was a Jewish leader who was appointed by the Persian government to return to the land of Israel and rebuild it as a Jewish country. While this was a joyous event that signaled the conclusion of the children of Israel's 70-year exile, this request came with many challenges. The locals in Israel at the time, who had been placed there by the Babylonians when they conquered Israel, were not so excited about the prospect of the Jewish people coming home. They made all sorts of problems for the returning Jews. They caused all kinds of opposition to fulfilling this charge. At one point, it looked as though Zerubbabel might fail at his task. Many of our tasks seem doomed from the beginning, but the Lord will help you conquer those mountains—to defeat those things that seem impossible. But, with God all things are possible!

Day 46

WHEN GOD SEEMS SILENT

Although sometimes God seems silent, He is always near. When I can't hear his voice or feel His presence, I know that He is still here. When He seems silent, I know by faith that it means there is more to come for me. It may seem quiet where you are too. Maybe you too can feel God's silence. Keep in mind that God's promise to Abraham is his promise to you and me, as well:

Genesis 28:15
> *"Behold I am with you and will keep you wherever you go, and will bring you back to this land; for I will not leave you until I have done what I have spoken to you." (NKJV)*

God is saying that He will not leave us until He has finished giving us everything He has promised to us. That is a promise we can trust because God doesn't lie. That is the assurance that we have. Simply stand on His word because His Word is true and He will not fail us. It's only a matter of time your heart will be strangely and tremendously moved. Your ears will hear the voice of God again. Your soul will feel His presence.

Ludwig van Beethoven wrote most of his most memorable music after he went deaf. He couldn't even hear the applause of the audience. He wrote the fantastic "Fate Symphony"—The 5th Symphony—while deaf. One of his most endearing sonatas, *The Moonlight Sonata* was written when he was deaf. These are personal favorites of mine among some others. It is remarkable that he was able to capture such beautiful music while he was deaf. The music was still on the inside of him. This is much like when God seems silent to us, our faith should be able to sustain us while we are waiting on God to act. When the music stops and God seems distant, sing acappella.

When God seems silent is when we should remember His word and His promises to us. This should keep us. Also, when God seems silent, we can gain strength by learning from our bad situations. Most of all we should remember that God says that 'He will always be with us and keep us wherever we go and wherever we are.' There is no reason to fear! When God is silent, we can rely on our knowledge that God will come through for us. Don't ever give up on God.

Day 47

GOD WILL CARRY YOU THROUGH

Deuteronomy 1:30–31
(30) "The Lord your God, who is going before you, will fight for you, as he did for you in Egypt, before your very eyes, (31) and in the wilderness. There you saw how the Lord your God carried you, as a father carries his son, all the way you went until you reached this place."

God is going before you and with you through the storms and the rains, the pitfalls and the obstacles, the bad situations of life and the negative places, to the mountain tops and in the valleys, through the uncertainties of life, in troubled relationships, through sickness and pain, through heartache and emptiness, through spiritually depleted times, and through emotional experiences. God is with us before, during, and after these moments.

God was with Israel during their plight in Egypt. He was with them as they were delivered from bondage. He was with them throughout their wilderness experience. He was with them after they were at their place of destiny. Just like in this passage, and others, God is always with you! He carries you as a father carries his son or daughter. God has not left you alone. He has often stated in His word that He will never leave us or forsake us until the end of the age.

During Moses' uncertainties he was able to carry out his call to a mission even though he was unable to speak well (Exod 4:10ff). But, God was with him and He did do the work of the Lord.

Yes, the Lord is also with us during times of sadness,

sickness, and even death. He becomes our source of comfort, peace, hope, and encouragement to go onward during such time in life. God will carry us through.

Day 48

CLAIM YOUR PROMISED LAND

Deuteronomy 2:36–37
(36) From Aroer on the rim of the Arnon Gorge, and from the town in the gorge, even as far as Gilead, not one town was too strong for us. The Lord our God gave us all of them. (37) But in accordance with the command of the Lord our God, you did not encroach on any of the land of the Ammonites, neither the land along the course of the Jabbok nor that around the towns in the hills.

There are challenges to be the most successful, the richest, and the biggest. Churches also fall prey to such competition, contending to be the church with the largest membership and the best at everything. There are instances today where one ministry is working in competition against another. God has something for each of us to do. Everyone has a niche, and we must find that place and dwell in it. Each of us was made for something wonderful and unique. Find that place and strive to achieve it. Learn from others; but, always remember that there is only one you. You are unique!

Be satisfied in being the best you that you can be. The Lord will help you accomplish your goals. All you have to do is to trust Him to guide you. Reach for your blessings a little at a time, each day.

Day 49

THE LORD IS NEAR TO THE BROKENHEARTED

Psalm 34:18
> *The Lord is close to the brokenhearted and saves those who are crushed in spirit.*

If the truth be told, most of us would rather avoid the bad, painful, and distasteful experiences in our lives. Who wouldn't? No one likes to live through pain and suffering. It hurts! Wouldn't it be wonderful if we could just skip over these unpleasant moments in our lives? But, we can't. What should happen is that we should learn that God is close to us to save us and He specializes in tending to the brokenhearted and saves us when are bruised. Hurts and pain require a spiritual solution.

When King David wrote Psalm 34, he was facing danger in his life but he was miraculously saved! He wrote, "The Lord is close to the brokenhearted and saves those who are crushed in spirit." We can get closest to God in our moments of deep depression, inner turmoil, crushed spirit, and emotional pain because God is closest to us in these times and brings complete salvation. Our greatest victories can come at these times!

Who wouldn't want to get close to God at our most helpless moments? During these moments we must:

1. Pray and communicate with God;
2. Study and remember God's word;
3. Become rooted and grounded in faith, confidence, and trust in God (see verse 7 where David knew that the

Lord's angels were encamped all about him);

4. During challenging times, always listen for the voice of God. During the nighttime, the Lord says, "weeping may last for the night, but joy comes in the morning time" (Ps 30:5); and

5. Praise the Lord during the bad times, as well as good times—praise Him at *all* times.

Psalm 34:1
   "I will bless the Lord at all times, and His praises shall be continually be in my mouth."

Remember, God is always near.

Day 50

SPIRITUAL WARFARE: ON BATTLING THE DEVIL

When you are living in covenant with God, you can stand on the blessings of Deuteronomy 28. One of them deals specifically with spiritual warfare:

Deuteronomy 28:7
   "The Lord will cause your enemies who rise against you to be defeated before your face; they shall come out against you one way and flee before you seven ways."

Kingdom believers must learn how to discern demonic strategies against their life, and how to break free from the enemy's stranglehold. Satan does not want you to know about spiritual warfare. The passage from Deuteronomy is really a covenant blessing. God has promised that He will cause our enemies who rise up against us to be defeated before our faces. Do your part by pursuing the following:

1. Diligently obey the voice of the Lord your God. In order to see this blessed promise come to pass in your life, you need to understand it in context; read the entire chapter of Deuteronomy 28. The first verse of that chapter clearly states, "Now it shall come to pass, if you diligently obey the voice of the Lord your God, to observe carefully all His commandments which I command you today…"

2. Repent before you engage in battle. We have all sinned and fall short of the glory of God.

3. Know that God is on your side. In Exodus 15:3, the children of Israel knew where they stood and where God stood. After the great deliverance from Egypt, they declared in song, "The Lord is a man of war; the Lord is His name." They knew that, "The Lord shall go forth like a mighty man; He shall stir up His zeal like a man of war. He shall cry out, yes, shout aloud; He shall prevail against His enemies" (Isa 42:13). They knew that the battle belongs to the Lord (1 Sam 17:47). They understood that they were God's battleaxe and weapons of war (see Jer 51:20).

4. Go to war from a position of victory. When Goliath challenged the army of Israel, the soldiers were scared witless of the Philistine champion. But David was a covenant man and he understood that victory belonged to Him in God. As a believer, know the victory is yours.

5. Praise your way through. In the Song of Moses in Exodus 15:2, the children of Israel sang a song to the

Lord that went something like this: "The Lord is my strength and song, and He has become my salvation; He is my God, and I will praise Him; my father's God, and I will exalt Him." Of course, that was after Israel's deliverance from Egypt. If you want to make the devil flee, praise God before you engage in battle. Praise brought down the walls at Jericho (Joshua 6) and praise gave Jehoshaphat victory in battle ("Now when they began to sing and to praise, the Lord set ambushes against the people of Ammon, Moab, and Mount Seir, who had come against Judah; and they were defeated"; 2 Chr 20:22).

6. Take up your armor. We all know God has given us His armor, as outlined in Ephesians 6. But how many of us actually put it on before running to the battle line? Get a revelation of the belt of truth, the breastplate of righteousness, the shoes of peace, the shield of faith, the helmet of salvation, and the sword of the spirit. Take some time to understand what this really means as part of your covenant with God. Satan cannot defeat the obedient soldier of God who is armored up and ready to fight. He'll likely flee toward someone who is undressed—unrepentant, or uninformed about our covenant.

7. Pray always and be watchful.

8. Resist the devil, and he will flee from you (James 4:7)!

Day 51

GOD AND HIS AGENDA IS PRIORITY #1

Matthew 6:33
"But seek first the Kingdom of God and His righteousness, and all these things shall be added to you." (NKJV)

Your will be done! That is the way in which we must live our lives. When we do that, we can rest assured that everything else will fall into place for us. Many people do not give God the proper respect in their lives, rather thinking selfishly, thinking of themselves. God has declared that He is a jealous God and doesn't want us to put anything before Him. What is your priority today? Sometimes the cares of life keep us from thinking on God. Sometimes the priorities of trying to make ends meet and make sense of life keep us from giving God the devotion that should be given to Him. Remember to go to bed with prayer and adoration to God and wake up to prayer and devotion to Almighty God. He deserves it! Let's bless the Lord at all times. Give Him praise and honor, even when things are not going as well as we would like. Always bless His name! Think on God and everything else will fall into proper perspective for us.

Priorities tend to rule our lives, and God's will fades into the background of our heart and mind. Why not make God the number one priority. Consistently keep prayer, worship, and praise at the forefront of your mind. That is what the popular phrase "put God first" means. Don't let that become a cliché to you. Always spend time with the Lord! Always keep Him on your mind!

As you spend time with God daily, He will be always

near to you. What happens is that the more time we spend with God the more God's priorities take precedence in our lives. Who will shape your priorities today? Will it be God or something or someone else? What priority will take precedence for you today? God wants us to take care of our business, but He also wants us to put him first in all things.

Matthew 6:9-10
> *"In this manner, therefore, pray: Our Father in heaven, hallowed be Your name. "Your kingdom come. Your will be done on earth as it is in heaven." (NKJV)*

"Your will be done."

Day 52

ON FOLLOWING CHRIST

Where Jesus leads me, I will follow. Anywhere. Anytime.

Jesus' inner circle during His earthly ministry followed Him everywhere He went. They had to walk everywhere they went—the dusty and rocky roads, to the mountaintops, in the valleys, to Galilee, Jerusalem, Samaria, and other hamlets being taught by Jesus and assisting Him in ministering to the needs of people. They witnessed His miracles: They were there when Jesus fed the thousands, healed the blind and lame, attended the wedding at Cana, they were even with Him in His prayer time and solicitude, and in the midst of suffering. They walked with Him. They learned from Him. They made their home with Him! They left their homes and trades to walk with Christ! Day after day they followed Christ.

Christ invites you to follow Him today.   Do you have a personal relationship with Him? Will you follow Christ today? The hymn writer says, 'where He leads me, I will follow—I'll go with Him, with Him, all the way.'

Day 53

SHOULD BELIEVERS BE "NICE" AND TOLERANT?

We hear so much about tolerance in this day in time or being politically correct. When are we to speak, and when –if at all—are we to be silent? Is it possible to witness and never say anything as a follower of Christ? Are we never to say anything about the wrongs or evils in the world? The prophets of old spoke out concerning the evils of their day, in government, community, and in religious circles. Then, why are we expected to remain quiet in a day when everything is said that is anti-Christian, but Christians are told to be silent or "Don't Judge"—be quiet! Let things go. The Church and pastors are told what they can and cannot do or say.

Tolerance is the watchword of the day in today's society. *What is tolerance?* Tolerance may be defined as "the ability to accept, experience, or survive something harmful or unpleasant," and "willingness to accept feelings, habits, or beliefs that are different from your own." The world desires for the Christian's response to be acceptance of anything the world offers and to not say anything against it.

To tolerate something is different than to allow something, because the word "allow" means that you are in a position of authority and could be in some measure responsible for the outcome of a situation. To tolerate something is to bear or endure something that you don't necessarily have control over or that you don't believe in. What is meant by "being nice" is being accommodating to worldliness and sin. So essentially, "being nice" in this instance isn't being nice at all, but rather destructive. One of the major problems of today is that far too many Christians are aiding and abetting the cause of Satan by supporting his program. Tolerating things contrary to God's will is no different from opening the door to evil and sin in our own lives.

The most important question is 'what does Jesus Christ expect of us believers?' Further, what should we as Christians tolerate? How should Christians handle today's problems? A Christian should in no way compromise the gospel of Jesus Christ. Any means of opening the door to sin and evil should be avoided; this would include being politically correct and accommodating evil doctrines & philosophies.

It's been mentioned before of the importance of being a true follower of Jesus Christ...This begs the question, 'what is Jesus like?' There seems to be a created dichotomy between a nice Jesus versus an intolerant Jesus. Let's look at whether or not Jesus Christ is nice (or accommodating, cooperative) and compromising when it comes to sin. Let's look to where the main proof is, the Word of God. There we see that Jesus is evidently intolerant when it comes to sin and unrighteousness. For example, He wasn't nice or tolerant when confronted by those "money-changers" in the temple, desecrating the Temple of God. It is recorded when He confronted the "money changers" that He used violence. This Jesus saw the money changers in the temple and He was not polite about it. He was downright intolerant. He fashioned a whip (this is what the lawyers would call 'premeditation') and physically drove the merchants away. He turned over tables and shouted. He caused a scene.

John 2:15
> *So he made a whip out of cords, and drove all from the temple courts, both sheep and cattle; he scattered the coins of the money changers and overturned their tables.*

Believers in the "nice Jesus" disregard the scriptures where He displays anger to those who were "money-changing" in the temple. Or of His/God's wrath in Old Testament. They only look at the scriptures where He was a friend to prostitutes and sinners. We must look at both sides of an issue; the Bible *and* common sense should be our guide. Jesus in fact condemned. He denounced. He caused trouble. He disrupted the established order. He was revolutionary! His moral laws were different from the status quo. God does not compromise when it comes to wrong and injustice. Being a Christian doesn't equate to cooperating with evil in the world by either not saying anything, taking action, being passive, and submissive to injustice.

Day 54

ENJOYING GOD'S WORLD THE RIGHT WAY - PART ONE

Psalm 24:1-2
(1) The earth is the Lord's, and everything in it, the world, and all who live in it; (2) for he founded it upon the seas and established it upon the waters.

Psalm 104:14-15
(14) He makes grass grow for the cattle, and plants for man to cultivate—bringing forth food from the earth: (15) wine that gladdens the heart of man, oil to make his face shine, and bread that sustains his heart.

The earth produces a feast. It not only produces necessities, but also luxuries. By the aid of the sun, moon, and rain, the earth provides for the needs and enjoyment of mankind. People are sometimes not a good steward or custodian of what God is given. Verse 15 of Psalm 104, 'wine that makes glad the heart of man'—how wonderful it would be if people were wise enough to know how to use this gladdening product of the vine; but, alas, he often turns it to ill account, and debases himself therewith. He gets drunk and commits atrocities of various kinds. Learn to be a good steward of what God has provided. Humanity bears the blame for what happens as a result of its lack of stewardship or (deliberate) harmful plans resulting in poor results.

"…And oil to make his face to shine."

Eastern peoples use oil more than we do in the western hemisphere. They delight in anointing with perfumed oils and regard the shining of the face as a choice emblem of joy. God is to be praised for all the products of the soil. He is the one who causes them to grow.

"…And bread which strengthens man's heart."

People have more courage after they are fed; many a depressed spirit have been comforted by a good substantial meal. We feel better! Bless and give praise to God for strength of heart as well as our physical sustenance. All that we have and enjoy are bounties of the kindness of God. Because of God we have abundant blessings!

God created a world bursting with vibrant colors, tastes, textures, and aromas. He created animals so unusual, perfectly beautiful, and distinct from one another. He created gorgeous roses and stunning sunsets. God has made us a wondrous world. Why? Because He does not want us to merely 'get through' life; He wants us to enjoy our lives and celebrate each day. Will you celebrate today? Let us be good stewards of God's world and enjoy it the right way.

Day 55

THOUGHTS ON ENJOYING GOD'S WORLD - PART TWO

I love the great outdoors. It has aesthetic value for me and puts me in touch with God when I observe the beauty of nature—of how well the planet was put together. Nature also puts me in touch with myself. I enjoy the beauty of God's creation—its music, art, sculpture, and the elements. God has given us the best of everything in this world to enjoy and prosper. He gave us provisions to sustain us for our daily living. God has painted beautiful scenes for our enjoyment and created wholesome food for our nourishment. When used appropriately all that God has given us is for our good.

Being good stewards of what He has put into our hands is to use constraints and restraints, such as abstaining from wine for the selfish craving of getting drunk and satisfying our fleshly lusts. Salvation means that an individual chooses to take upon himself or herself abide by such constraints when enjoying what God has provided for us. Let us not misuse what God has given us (see Pss 24:1-2; 104:14-15).

Day 56

ON THE CHRISTIAN LIFESTYLE

Christ being our Redeemer is the starting point for the Christian lifestyle. He is Holy and expects us to be holy also. He is our Portrait (our mirror image) which means that we look to Him as an example. Christ is Lord, Savior, Deliverer, Redeemer, Strength, and Power.

My personal testimony is that I have always tried to live for the Lord, ever since I was a teenager. I am 'human,' but I endeavored to be one who would try to be an example of what I preached, sang, and testified about. I was (and still am) simply determined to be a living example of what I preached. To me that is the greatest teacher of all—an example of someone trying to live up to the principles of Christ.

It may not have been easy all the time, but I was always determined to not be like what I saw around me from people and preachers all over the area who pretended to be holy, but lived differently. There are many who view this life in Christ as if it is entertainment or a business venture. Some act as if they are rock stars!

I hear several young people today asking the question: 'Is there anyone trying to live according to the principles of the Bible today?' or, 'Is the Bible still relevant today for Christians?' Many people have been convinced that 'being human,' God understands, and therefore, He authorizes actions contrary to His will. This really suggests that God's Word cannot be entirely trusted, and thus can be amended. However, God cannot be wrong. He foreknew everything from the beginning of time. Christ came all the way from heaven down to earth to be a living epistle—a living example of how to revere God even in our humanity—in the flesh. *You* should be a living epistle. God created us to be moral agents. Morality is the standard; it honors God. Also, as you remain in the will of God the Holy Spirit will sanctify you daily. In a sense, you are in a process of "becoming." Do not allow your flesh impede the work of the Holy Spirit.

Prominent figures from scripture committed great offenses, such as David (psalmist and king, yet philandered), Peter (curser and slasher), and Thomas (had doubts and uncertainties about the resurrection). With that, remember that the Lord is a forgiver of sins, mistakes, and errors. Isn't it good to know that we serve a God like that?

Jesus Christ is the Chief Cornerstone of the Body. Look to Jesus, the author and finisher of your faith. As the hymn says, "To be like Jesus, O how I want to be like Him!" Strive to please the Lord in every way, no matter what—no playing games, no hypocrisy, no compromise. Lift up the name of Jesus through living a life of love, respect, goodness, and integrity. That is what it really means to be saved—a true Christian and a true child of God. Apostle John (12:32, NKJV) wrote these words spoken by Lord Jesus: "And I, if I am lifted up from the earth, will draw all *peoples* to Myself."

Day 57

THE PARABLE OF THE TALENTS AND SERVANTS

Matthew 25:16-18
(16) The man who had received the five talents went at once and put his money to work and gained five more. (17) So also, the one with the two talents gained two more. (18) But the man who had received the one talent went off, dug a hole in the ground and hid his master's money.

The servants of the master in this parable did not know how long their master would be gone, so two of them went about doing their best to use their talents to make more money. One of them decided to procrastinate while the Master was gone away. Just maybe, he also was distraught that he didn't receive but one talent. People today feel like if they don't have much they shouldn't make any effort to give of themselves or their substance. The Followers of Christ should have the attitude that they will use their talents to the best of their ability, no matter what. Scripture states that we should 'work while it is day because night is coming.' The Lord wants His followers to work in His vineyard and be productive. Using our gifts or talents means to serve others and witness for the Lord. We must work each day as if it is our last day. Christ will be glorified and the people of God will be blessed. When our gifts are used to the honor and glory of God, people will be blessed and God will be glorified!

The word "talents" in this parable refers to money. It's a good investment to invest the Master's money in the product of souls and a good witness for Jesus Christ! The word talent in our modern language refers to skills and abilities of individuals. The diligent servants in this parable went right to work, no doubt with gladness. The servant with the five talents increased his by 100% and also the one with the two talents. Their original assets were doubled. This is a good lesson that the more we work, the more blessed we will become. The servant with the one talent did not receive any return on his money, because he failed to do anything with the one talent that he had. If he would have worked, even though he only had one talent, he still would have received at least a 100% increase as well. The point is that no matter what we have to offer, it should be rendered to the glory and honor of God. When we are diligent with what we have the Lord will bless us accordingly. Little becomes much when placed in the Master's hands.

The motivation to work and be productive should be based on the love for the Master or the object of our service. When we love God, we will work for Him because He is God, and not be concerned about our rewards. The rewards will come when we work in love. The servant with the one talent didn't display love for his master or himself. Sadly, he failed to trade with his talent and multiply it. Fearing his master's severity, he wrapped his lord's asset in a handkerchief and hid it in a hole in the earth. Fear is a sad thing when a person dreads losing something valuable so much that he hoards it instead of putting it to good use. So it is with a spiritual gift also.

While His fellow servants were actively trading their talents, the third servant was idle. He was neither actively obedient nor disobedient, but passively disobedient. He did not intend to hurt his master's property; he simply failed to improve it. He did nothing! Similar to the foolish virgins suffering because they neglected to prepare, the third servant in this parable suffers because he did nothing with his talent. We must not hide our light under a basket. The Bible declares that we are the light of the world and the salt of the earth and a city that sits on a hill—a light shining in a dark world. Let your light shine so that people may see your good works and glorify the Father in heaven (Matt 5:1-16)!

Day 58

BROKENNESS... ACCEPTING WHAT GOD ALLOWS

Matthew 26:38-39
(38) Then he said to them, "My soul is overwhelmed with sorrow to the point of death. Stay here and keep watch with me." (39) Going a little farther, he fell with his face to the ground and prayed, "My Father, if it is possible, may this cup be taken from me. Yet not as I will, but as you will."

This text captures Jesus Christ in His humanity. He displays similar emotions that we feel and face from time to time. Jesus was in agony. He was suffering inner turmoil. He is our example of how to get through life's toughest moments. Now that we have the Spirit of God available to us, we can make it through! The Holy Spirit gives us strength. Apostle Paul states in Philippians 4:13, "I can do everything through Christ who gives me strength."

At the point in the Matthew text above, Jesus had accepted His fate. But in His state of sorrow and facing impending death, He had a desire to avoid the bitter cup if at all possible but resigned Himself to following the will of the Father rather than His own. Whenever we are facing sorrow and despair or brokenness of any kind, it is a very uncomfortable position to be in and very frightening. Accept what God allows and stand firm like Job when he declared, "all of my appointed time will I wait until my change comes." Until my change comes… Hold steady to the promises of Jesus Christ.

When your spirit is broken there is a feeling of being overwhelmed with sorrow to the point of death. When problems seem insurmountable, it is impossible to absorb the worst of events in your life. But it simply takes faith in moments like these to simply know that what is to come is greater than the trouble you are facing. Have a meeting of the minds with the Lord; speak to Him as openly as a friend, yet humbly as before a king. You must simply stand firm in the midst of trouble and say to the Lord, 'not my will but *Your* will be done.'

Day 59

NEVER ALONE

Jesus Christ Moves by the Holy Spirit

The Lord promised to send us help. We are never alone (Heb 13:5)! He promised never to abandon us. The Lord is our comforter through the Holy Spirit. He is always reminding us of the Word of God and His mercy. The Holy Spirit is always on the job. I remember a time when I was driving home in my first car from my first teaching position in Interlachen, Florida, when suddenly I ended up on the side of the road in a ditch to avoid a serious accident. I talked with myself all the way home saying 'be careful from now on and slow down.' The Holy Spirit provided protection, guided the steering wheel, and steered me to safety. I thank God for the unceasing presence of the Holy Spirit.

I am determined to hear the voice of the Holy Spirit because it is in Him that we live, move, and have our being. The Lord promised in His word (Matt 28:20b), "I am with you always, to the very end of the age." The Holy Spirit is a great gift from God. The Holy Spirit along with the Father and the Son are forever cheering for us. When we are in a jam, the Holy Spirit is there. When we need someone to talk to, the Holy Spirit is there. When we need solace, serenity, and peace, the Holy Spirit is there with us. We are never alone. No, never alone.

John 15:26
> *"But when the Helper comes, whom I will send to you from the Father, the Spirit of truth, who proceeds from the Father, He*

Day 60

FREEDOM FROM ANXIETY AND DEPRESSION

Luke 8:22-25

(22) One day Jesus said to his disciples, "Let's go over to the other side of the lake." So they got into a boat and set out. (23) As they sailed, he fell asleep. A squall came down on the lake, so that the boat was being swamped, and they were in great danger. (24) The disciples went and woke him, saying, "Master, Master, we're going to drown!" He got up and rebuked the wind and the raging waters; the storm subsided, and all was calm. (25) "Where is your faith?" Jesus asked his disciples. In fear and amazement they asked one another, "Who is this? He commands even the winds and the water, and they obey him."

The prospect of raising children and training them to become responsible, wholesome, God fearing adults seems to be growing dimmer. Satan has launched an extensive campaign to capture the minds of our youth. More than one-third of marriages in this country alone end in divorce. Children are brought up in homes with one parent. These and other problems have caused the minds of men and women to be infiltrated with anxiety and depression leading to many committing suicide. Even pastors have been committing suicide. Church members are suffering depression. People are losing faith in surviving the cares of life, thus they are losing faith in God. Some feel like suicide is the answer and because of these pressures, men and women, boys and girls are turning to drugs and alcohol, having nervous breakdowns, have heart trouble, and ulcers. In many areas of life there seems to be good reasons for pessimism and helplessness. Internationally, it appears that lasting peace will never be attained. Nationally, there is racial, political, and economic chaos on a constant brink of eruption.

Follower of Christ, do not be upset and disturbed by all of the turbulence and trouble in the world. Do not be troubled and perplexed as those who do not know Christ. With the power of the Holy Spirit, you have the strength and internal fortitude to conquer all those demons. But one must trust Christ for real and believe that He is the reward for those who diligently seek Him. The impossible becomes the possible. The Holy Spirit soothes all tension, calms the nerves, heals the broken heart, and brings stability to your entire being (mind, soul and spirit.)

Fear and anxiety gripped the hearts of the disciples. Christ in one's life should make all the difference. May you remember that through Christ, you can do all things! The power of the Holy Spirit soothes your doubts and fears. It may not be easy to do when we are going through, but keep on believing and trusting in Christ and He will give you victory.

Day 61

RESPECT FOR GOD, HIS SON, HIS WORD, HIS CHURCH

1 Peter 2:1-3
(1) Therefore, rid yourselves of all malice and all deceit, hypocrisy, envy, and slander of every kind. (2) Like newborn babies, crave pure spiritual milk, so that by it you may grow up in your salvation, (3) now that you have tasted that the Lord is good.

1 Peter 2:9
But you are a chosen people, a royal priesthood, a Holy nation, a people belonging to God, that you may declare the praises of Him who called you out of darkness into His wonderful light.

The Lord wants you to know that you are of a chosen people, a royal priesthood, and a Holy nation. You belong to God. You are no longer your own, but you have been bought with the price of Jesus' blood and suffering. He called you out of 'darkness of sin and into the marvelous light of holiness.' God chose you! Galatians 5:1 says to us to 'stand fast in the liberty where Christ has set us free and be not entangled again with the yoke of bondage.' We are free in Jesus, but this freedom does not give us a license to sin. It is because of God's grace and mercy that we are saved and have life; therefore; we must give due respect to God in our lives. We do not have the right to treat the things of God any kind of way. We must respect and honor Him in every way.

There is a move today that would make a person think that it's alright to do almost anything under the sun. Whatever happened to following the precepts of Almighty

God in public and in private? As Christians, live as honest moral beings as God requires, not disregarding God's will; such a person recklessly assumes to be on a path toward heaven regardless of the lifestyle. Don't be a living contradiction, taking on the title of 'Christian,' yet not revering God, His Word, or His Son's supreme sacrifice. He gave His life for your salvation, and to be set free indeed.

Day 62

JESUS CHRIST, THE ISLE OF STABILITY

Malachi 3:6
"For I am the Lord, I do not change; therefore you are not consumed, O sons of Jacob."

The world is full of turmoil and uncertainties from day to day. Many times we do not know where to turn. But, the *only* sure thing is that Christ is the same yesterday, today, and forever. He doesn't change. We need a focal point for our lives. Jesus is it!

Stability is needed in life; people are always looking for it, sometimes in all the wrong places. People try to reach the pinnacle of peace and solace through drugs, sex, shopping, sports, education, and more; albeit, nothing seems to satisfy the inner peace. People may not be aware of it, but since the beginning of time, humanity has had a hunger for inner peace. That hunger has taken humanity on a quest for personal freedom from century to century. The antidote for anxiety, pain, and trouble is Jesus Christ.

Nothing can bring stability and peace like Jesus Christ can. We need something *stable* and *certain* and *sure* in our lives! The Lord God is immutable (unchanging). God's *Word* never changes. When we stand on it, it is a sure foundation. It is a futile and unnecessary thing to try to change the Word of God—the Bible—and God Himself, because none of these things will ever change. Fact is, there can be *no* lasting peace without Jesus Christ.

Our "Isle of Stability" is Christ, the Solid Rock. Our certainty in uncertain and troubling times is Christ. He is our Fortress, our Foundation, our Peace, and our Hope.

Day 63

HOW MANY TIMES WILL YOU FALL FOR SATAN'S LIES?

Satans lies have been going on from the Garden of Eden until now. He has unleashed his plot in every age of history. It has caused nations to fall, people to be destroyed, and pain and suffering to be endured all over the world. His lies are about getting people to live independently of God, fulfilling the lust of the flesh, denouncing God. People become self-centered in making themselves and their pleasures as the main reason for living—their wants, needs, plans all become their reasons for living. With this comes emptiness, dissatisfaction, pain, suffering, discontent—you name it! Why? The answer is because you have allowed Satan to dismiss God from your life.

Satan is subtle and slick in his plan to overtake you. He

tears down relationships, stops you from worshipping, praising, and serving God. It happens before you know it! He is a liar and a deceiver. Satan's lies are dispelled when you come to realize that the very thing you believe brings you pleasure is the thing to destroy you. God's Word informs us that Satan comes to steal, kill, and destroy.

Guard your heart, guard your mind, and guard your soul. Pursue prayer and supplication, fasting, Bible study, fellowship with believers, attend church, listen to anointed word and music, and stay on top of Satan's tactics.

Genesis 3:1
> *"Now the serpent was craftier than any of the wild animals the Lord God had made. He said to the woman, "Did God really say, 'You must not eat from any tree in the garden'?"*

Satan is crafty just like the serpent. He deceived Eve into eating from a forbidden tree in the Garden of Eden. You must be aware of Satan's tactics!

John 10:10
> *"The thief comes only to steal and kill and destroy; I have come that they may have life, and have it to the full."*

Satan is a thief and a robber—His intention is to bring destruction to your life. But there is *abundant* life in Jesus Christ.

Romans 12:1-2
> *(1) Therefore, I urge you, brothers, in view of God's mercy, to offer your bodies as living sacrifices, holy and pleasing to God— this is your spiritual act of worship. (2) Do not conform any longer to the pattern of this world, but be transformed by the renewing of your mind. Then you will be able to test and approve what God's will is—his good, pleasing and perfect will.*

135

Paul makes a strong appeal to believers to strive to be holy. Both the Old and New Testaments consistently admonish God's children to be holy. Believers must live for the Lord and not fall for Satan's lies. The Followers of Christ must not water down the truth of the Word of God. Paul makes a strong and urgent appeal to Christians to devote their lives to sacrifice—that is, giving up the world—and following Jesus wholeheartedly. This is the way to avoid Satan's lies and deceptions. Jesus Christ made the supreme sacrifice for us when He gave up His life for our complete and total salvation. Maintain your salvation through holiness; this pleases God and helps you not fall prey to satanic forces. God wants you to be holy just like Him. You must give yourself to God completely through His Son, Jesus Christ. This is an honorable thing to do if we truly love the Lord! We show that we value our life in Christ and place value on the things of God. Therefore, the apostle Paul is urging those of us who have had a revelation of God and a real experience with God to devote ourselves entirely and earnestly to living out this revelation of God in our lives. If we do this, Satan will not cause us to fall for his lies.

We must sacrifice our bodies—our entire being—including our hearts, minds, souls, and spirits to God. We must render our character, attitudes, perspectives, experiences, energy, knowledge, skills, and abilities to the Father through Christ. Everything about us must be surrendered to the Lord with nothing held back.

Day 64

BEING GOD'S WORKMANSHIP

Ephesians 1:3-6
(3) Praise be to God and Father of our Lord Jesus Christ, who has blessed us in the heavenly realms with every spiritual blessing in Christ. (4) For He chose us in Him before the creation of the world to be holy and blameless in His sight. In love (5) He predestined us to be adopted as His sons through Jesus Christ, in accordance with His pleasure and will—(6) to the praise of His glorious grace, which He has freely given us in the One He loves.

God the Father has claimed believers from the foundation of the world to be His sons, daughters, and joint heirs to His promise of salvation and eternal life. It is His intention that, as believers, we be like Him. Our adoption by God gives us a relationship with Him and positions us in a *special* place as His sons and daughters. This is an honorable place to be in God. It must not be taken lightly! I think that many times we forget that we have a special place in God—a relationship that creates a bond with Him. That's what we were created for—a close relationship with God. As His heirs to the promise, He has chosen us to be *'Holy and blameless'* in God's sight.

God created us after His will from the foundation of the world. He formed us in His image and likeness. . . In Genesis chapter one, God created man on the sixth day of the creation of the world, and gave him dominion over the entire earth.

Genesis 1:26-27
(26) Then God said, "Let us make man in Our image, in Our

likeness, and let them rule over the fish of the sea and the birds of the air, over the livestock, over all the earth, and over all the creatures that move along the ground." (27) So God created man in His own image, in the image of God He created him; male and female He created them.

God put man into a place of esteem and supplied him with all that he needed to survive. He even gave man free will—the freedom to choose. But, God also provided a way for man to live close to God through His Son, Jesus Christ.

Day 65

BEING CHRIST'S WORKMANSHIP

Ephesians 1:22-23
(22) And God placed all things under His feet (Christ) and appointed Him to be head over everything for the church, (23) which is His body, the fullness of Him who fills everything in every way.

This verse places Christ over each of us—His body to develop and lead. The Church of God is placed 'under Christ's feet' and the people therein. We are His workmanship! God gives us a method of salvation through His Son, Jesus Christ. The word says,

Ephesians 2:1-3
(1) As for you, you were dead in your transgressions and sins, (2) in which you used to live when you followed the ways of this world and of the ruler of the kingdom of the air, the spirit who is now at work in those who are disobedient. (3) All of us also lived among

them at one time gratifying the cravings of our sinful nature and following its desires and thoughts.

We all used to be a part of the world, but God through Jesus Christ was rich in mercy and love and gave us a way to become members of the Body of Christ—it was by His love that He made us and gave us a place in His kingdom. The old sinful nature is gone and God's saving power is now a part of us through the Holy Spirit. God made us alive through Christ, even while we were yet dead in our transgressions. He loved us just that much! Christ is working on us continually by His Spirit for us to be true Children of God! The word of the Lord further states:

Ephesians 2:6-7
> *(6) And God raised us up with Christ and seated us with Him in the heavenly realms in Christ Jesus, (7) in order that in the coming ages He might show the incomparable riches of His grace, expressed in His kindness to us in Christ Jesus.*

Christ is consistently working on us to make us into what God through Christ wants us to be. We are becoming what He wants us to be every day. Verse 8 goes on to say that we have been saved by His grace and our faith in Christ. It is by simply believing in Christ that we receive salvation. Isn't that wonderful to receive the salvation of the Lord through our repentance? This is a marvelous gift from God!

Finally, Ephesians 2:10 gives us in a nutshell the plan of our salvation and the great gift God has given us:

> *For we are God's workmanship, created in Christ Jesus to do good works, which God prepared in advance for us to do.*

We have been saved and are being saved by grace through faith, by the gift of God. This means that we have a heritage with Christ and we should follow His lead and strive to be like Him and live like Him. Specifically, this means that we should be honoring Jesus; imitating Jesus; following Jesus; and obeying Jesus. Christ's workmanship should be:

> Thinking like Jesus thought.
> Living like Jesus lived.
> Walking like Jesus walked.
> Making disciples like Jesus made.
> Caring like Jesus cared.
> Sharing like Jesus shared.
> Giving like Jesus gave.
> Serving like Jesus served.

Day 66

DOES ANYTHING LAST FOREVER?

Ecclesiastes 1:2-4
> *(2) "Vanity of vanities," says the preacher; "Vanity of vanities, all is vanity." (3) What profit has a man from all his labor in which he toils under the sun? (4) One generation passes away, and another generation comes; but the earth abides forever. . . (NKJV)*

Malachi 3:5-6
> *(5) "And I will come near you for judgment; I will be a swift witness against sorcerers, against adulterers, against perjurers, against those who exploit wage earners and widows and orphans, and against those who turn away an alien—because they do not*

fear Me," says the Lord of hosts. (6) "For I am the Lord, I do not change; therefore you are not consumed, O sons of Jacob." (NKJV)

Everything around us changes: our friendships, relationships, money, jobs, health, etc. Everything! There is nothing certain or sure under the sun. There is a time and a season for everything. Solomon discovered in his old age that all of life was vain. Education, money and wealth, women (wives and concubines), power and positions, fortune and fame—all of life was vanity! Eating, drinking, and being merry only lasts for a while, then utter dismay, sadness, destruction, and yes, death! He found out that the only lasting things were the things of God! The things of God last forever!

The Word states, "But seek first the kingdom of God and His righteousness, and all these things shall be added to you. Therefore do not worry about tomorrow, for tomorrow will worry about its own things. Sufficient for the day is its own trouble" (Matt 6:33-34, NKJV). Nothing lasts forever, except the things of God. It is best to not put your trust in anything, other than God's promises. Colossians 3:20 states for us to set our affection on things above (God things), and not on things that are not lasting—things that will deteriorate—things that are not eternal.

Matthew 6:19-20
> *(19) "Do not lay up for yourselves treasures on earth, where moth and rust destroy and where thieves break in and steal; (20) "But lay up for yourselves treasures in heaven." (NKJV)*

Day 67

MAKE TODAY ABOUT JESUS—A JESUS DAY

Have your heart and mind set on Jesus Christ. The Bible states: 'Set your affection on things above and not on things of the earth' (Col 3:2).

Matthew 5:6
Blessed are those who hungry and thirst for righteousness, for they shall be filled. (NKJV)

Hunger and thirst for Jesus and make your day a Jesus filled day. Are you hungry or thirsty for Him?

Do you know what it's like to be thirsty? I remember when I was in the United States Army at Fort Benning, Georgia, I went on bivouac—a 30 mile walk in full gear. It was the middle of summer in Fort Benning and it was very hot. We only had three water breaks along the way for 20 minutes each. I was *so* thirsty and was glad to pull out that canteen and drink, no matter that it was not cold or with ice in it—it quenched my thirst. We could not drink it all at one stop, because we got no more along the way. With this realization, it was just good to have some water to drink. It was so satisfying to be able to get a drink of water! I you've been thirsty before. Can you remember what it was like to have a good refreshing glass of water? I certainly do! That's the way it should be with our love, adoration and desire for Jesus Christ! The Holy Bible describes God's promises to His people in this manner:

John 7:37-38
"Anyone who is thirsty may come to me! Anyone who believes in

me may come and drink! For the Scriptures declare, 'Rivers of living water will flow from his heart.'"

You can be a true believer and still be thirsty. Many times, we need to satisfy our thirst and hunger through Christ. We must live our lives connected to Christ and receive complete satisfaction just like drinking a glass of cool ice water. Jesus satisfies! Your soul will be satisfied by making your day and life all about Jesus. Is your soul satisfied today?

Day 68

ON FREE WILL

In the scheme of things today, God allows humans to exercise free will in living their lives…He does not tear the doors of our hearts down nor does He break into our hearts and souls! He allows us, since the Garden of Eden, to exercise free will.

Free will has taken a drastic turn in current times in that people are exercising it at a pace that is astronomical: redefining who God is, His Son, and even redefining the Holy Spirit! People have gotten so smart until they are even redefining God's Word, twisting it in all kinds of ways to mean what they want it to mean.

In a systematic theology class in seminary, I remember encountering this discussion and I understood that God is so loving until He didn't force His will or commands on mankind, but rather, allowed man to exercise His own desires. It means so much to God when we choose Him on our own.

God said in the Old Testament that He is a jealous God and that we should have *no other* gods above Him! Why is it that people think they know more than God or His Word? Children even think they know more than their parents, elders, or anyone who is in authority or more experienced! When I was a counselor at the State Prison System in Florida, the term they used for that was an authority problem and each prisoner in my group had to say if they were working on authority each day. Not too many people want to follow those in leadership over us, even God!

The idea of free will has gotten a lot of people in trouble and caused many of them to be destroyed way too young! God's Word is a light and a lamp to our feet and pathway! Why not follow His principles and precepts? This can curtail a lot of problems in our lives—doing things God's way!

We probably would do well to practice doing things God's way and it will curtail a myriad of problems in life. People often look at rules as a tremendous bother and heavy load that will cause them not to have fun any longer. But, it may just be to the contrary—it just may save you from having to pay a price in the future for something that was not thought out very well in the past or the now. God said, 'whosoever will let him come…' Let him come freely and voluntarily to the throne of grace! *Yes!* Free will also means exercising *good sense!* We are on the honor system! The only thing here is that God sees and knows the heart and mind of man. How will you use and exercise *your* free will today?

Day 69

GOD IS THE SAME YESTERDAY, TODAY, AND FOREVER

You have seen what the Lord has done in your life in the past, therefore; believe Him now for your future.

Deuteronomy 29:2-3
(2) Moses summoned all the Israelites and said to them: Your eyes have seen all that the LORD did in Egypt to Pharaoh, to all his officials and to all his land. (3) With your own eyes you saw those great trials, those miraculous signs and great wonders.

God is not far away—He is *so* near to you. You *must* remember that He is always around you whether you feel Him or not. He is there! The Israelite people had to be reminded of the great deeds that God had done for them in Egypt. It is amazing that they so easily forgot what God had done for them. But, they did! How many of us forget about what God has done for us in the past? We just don't remember that God brought us out many times and we should trust Him now no matter how bad the situation looks. Sometimes, we just need to be patient and trust God! God is the same yesterday, today, and forever!

Day 70

EVERY DAY IS FRESH AND NEW: A FRESH, NEW START

Around the country, America during certain times of the year get ready to go back to school. It is a time of excitement for students all over the country, from preschoolers to those who are seniors to those anticipating their final year of under graduate or post-graduate work, everyone is gearing up for another opportunity of learning. It is something fresh and exciting about starting all over again.

Each day we face is like that, it gives us a fresh start at moving towards success and the accomplishment of our dreams. Isn't it exciting? There is a line in a movie that talks about the beginning of school and freshly sharpened pencils and new notebooks and paper – there is something about the excitement of a fresh start. Are you excited about your life today? Your fresh start?

There is much excitement about the change of seasons. Some of us favor one season over another. Some love winter because of the winter sports, such as skiing. Others love the summer months because of the summer activities. Still others enjoy the spring time when the trees are turning green, the flowers are blooming, and temperature is mild—not too hot and not too cold. Everything is so bright and colorful. The autumn and fall the temperature changes and the leaves are very colorful—reds, yellows, browns, green, etc. and especially in the mountains and country sides, God's creation is so beautiful. I personally love many things about all of the seasons. I just love being alive and experience the variety of each new day, each new season, and each new year. I see each day as a fresh start to enjoy life. Enjoy God's world! Enjoy working for the Lord.

The book of Lamentations in the Bible has great truths about God's faithfulness that offers a fresh start daily …

Lamentations 3:22-23
> *(22) Because of the Lord's great love we are not consumed, for His compassions never fail. (23) They are new every morning; great is your faithfulness.*

Aren't you glad that God's compassion is new every morning? A fresh new start to life! Matthew provides another encouraging verse…

Matthew 6:34
> *Therefore do not worry about tomorrow, for tomorrow will worry about itself. Each day has enough trouble of its own.*

Thank God for the opportunity to be renewed and refreshed on a daily basis.

Day 71

PRIORITIES AND TIMING

Ecclesiastes 3:1-4, 11
> *(1) To everything there is a season, a time for every purpose under heaven: (2) A time to be born, and a time to die; a time to plant, and a time to pluck what is planted; (3) A time to kill, and a time to heal; a time to break down, and a time to build up; (4) A time to weep, and a time to laugh;; a time to mourn,*

and a time to dance; ... (11) He has made everything beautiful in its time... There is a time for everything and everything has its order of priority.

When it comes to the salvation of the Lord, the Word says 'now is the accepted time, now is the time or day of salvation.' That is the primary thing in all of life to seek God first. The Bible further states 'Seek first the Kingdom of God and His righteousness and all other things will be added unto you' (see Matt 6:33).

I ran across an old proverb that poses a question: When is the best time to plant a tree? The answer is 20 years ago. Then the question is asked, 'when is the second-best time to plant a tree?' The answer is now! Years down the road we will appreciate that we have planted seeds 20 years ago and is now producing. The other alternative is to start now while you still have life. We waste too much time placing priorities on things that do not count or are detrimental to our well-being. We spend a lot of time on trivial things, when things that really matter go lacking. Our success could have been achieved years ago while we meandered 'in the desert and wilderness of life' failing to reach our goals. Remember, the children of Israel wandered in the wilderness for 40 years and God never told them to do that. They simply made excuses and played the blame game to Moses and God. In one instance, they were afraid to get their feet wet, failing to step into the Jordan. The leaders were also afraid. Many times, we operate in fear as well, and blame others for what we should blame ourselves because we failed to follow through with instructions from God. Don't wait 20 years to plant a tree, because it will take about that time for it to grow and produce. If you missed doing it in the past, then <u>do it now</u>!

Priorities and timing are everything in planning to forge ahead in life. Take advantage of each new day to follow your goals and more importantly, the things of God.

Day 72

WHAT IS LOVE?

In the "Love Chapter" of 1 Corinthians 13:2 following that there is only two words provided for what love is—patient and kind. Aside from those two words, everything else describes what love is not—what love does not do, or what love does. Love is not jealous, love does not brag and is not arrogant, does not act unbecomingly; it does not seek its own, is not provoked, does not take into account a wrong suffered, does not rejoice in unrighteousness.

Love is patient and kind. Love requires much patience in order for it to be successful. A part of the beauty of love is the fact that a person can persevere through good times and bad times and never give up on love. It is patient! Real love is lasting and kind! Love is not whatever you want it to be, but love is patience—that is the essence of love—being able to love someone even when it is not so easy to do so. Patience means waiting because your heart says, I want this to work. This kind of love works! This kind of love does not fail!

The definition of love. Therefore, love is defined as patient and kind! When this is applied in a relationship, love will last! Real love works in a beautiful way when it is like that described in 1 Corinthians 13. This is the way love is supposed to work.

Love is a personal thing and love is relational. Love does not blame others, forget to listen, or fail to respect the other person. Put yourself into the other person's shoes. Love is more giving than taking. Christ actually moves a person to communicate and listen—to bear with, believe in, hope with, and endure together. Now, what do you think? How has the "Love Chapter" influenced the way you love others around you? Can you see true love from others from the characteristics listed in this passage? Do you think you can love and respect others better today?

Jesus displayed these qualities in dealing with us. While 'we were yet sinners, He died for us.' He exemplified love by showing *patience* and *kindness* towards us even in our sinful nature. Love is not to be taken lightly and this writer believes that love is the foundation for our salvation through God, and our source of good relationships to other people. The basic foundation of human relationships and our relationship to God is contingent upon our capacity to love.

Day 73

HAVE FAITH WHEN YOU PRAY

Worrying is at epidemic proportions. Even believers *worry* as if God is not real. I must confess that I have been a constant worrier, especially in the past! My wife used to remind me of my own sermons and repeat them back to me. Worry comes about because we personally have lost control; we have no control of many of the situations that we face in life. Peace and tranquility come about when *we* turn our situations over to God completely in faith! Now, this doesn't mean that we don't act in any way that we can by the strength of God, but simply that we act in *faith*.

Genesis 32:7
> *In great fear and distress Jacob divided the people who were with him into two groups, and the flocks and herds and camels as well.*

Most of the top ten prescribed drugs in America are to treat worry and its associated symptoms. Despite our tendency to worry, the human body was not created to worry. It's like using a car that was meant to transport groceries to haul cement. When we are anxious, we compromise our health, and our body functions at a fraction of its capability. I have heard it said that "worrying is the interest we pay on a debt we might not owe." Worry costs us good health, mental and emotional stability, spiritual serenity and abundant life!

Let us resolve to reduce our worry today! Will you?

Day 74

HOW TO BE SPIRITUALLY HEALTHY

1 Timothy 4:7-8
(7) Have nothing to do with godless myths and old wives' tales; rather, train yourself to be godly. (8) For physical training is of some value, but godliness has value for all things, holding promise for both the present life and the life to come.

The physical side of man has value and is important, but the spiritual life has value for all times—eternally. Your spiritual health is just as important for you as your physical health. It is important to practice those habits that will increase your spiritual stamina, like; praying, reading the Bible, fellowshipping with believers, and such like. Specifically, the life of Jesus Christ is the major example of what it will take to live a godly and spiritually healthy lifestyle. The disciples learned from Jesus about Scripture by listening to Jesus' teaching. They learned to pray by listening to Him pray and asking Him to teach them to pray. They learned to prioritize spending time with God by Jesus' example. They learned to abide in God's unconditional love as they experienced Jesus' love for them, and how to live in trusting relationships as they lived life together with Him and one another. Will you follow the lifestyle of Christ today for spiritual growth?

Apostle Paul taught Timothy how to develop his Christian lifestyle by having nothing to do with trivial pursuits and by not following myths and old wives' tales. He advised Timothy to 'train yourself to be godly.' It requires one to practice those things of God that will result in being closer to Him.

Paul further taught that the value of practicing godliness had significant values both in this present life and for the life to come. Will you practice godliness today and always?

Day 75

ON JUDGING THE UNGODLY

Jude 1:15-19
(15) ...to judge everyone, and to convict all the ungodly of all the ungodly acts they have done in the ungodly way, and of all the harsh words ungodly sinners have spoken against him." (16) These men are grumblers and faultfinders; they follow their own evil desires; they boast about themselves and flatter others for their own advantage. (17) But, dear friends, remember what the apostles of our Lord Jesus Christ foretold. (18) They said to you, "In the last times there will be scoffers who will follow their own ungodly desires." (19) These are the men who divide you, who follow mere natural instincts and do not have the Spirit.

We hear *so* much today about "do not judge" but this verse speaks clearly of just the opposite, when there is certainly evidence of ungodly ways being done even by ministry leaders. In this passage, we are instructed to avoid them, the reason being that this behavior can also contaminate those who are godly. This really is a warning so that the people of God can see how to avoid the traps of the enemy and live godly lives unto the Lord.

Verse 15 emphasizes the keyword ungodliness. There is nothing to be applauded about being ungodly! These false ministers mentioned here are the total opposites of what God is, and if we know what God is—what godliness is—then we can identify and avoid them, and not end up being a poor witness of what God is and what God requires for His people.

Jude gives four definitive descriptions to help us identify false teachers:

1. They are discontented murmurers and complainers. They always have something to gripe about. They are discontent with their lives and find fault about everything.
2. They live to satisfy their own selfish desires.
3. They speak bragging words
4. They are respecters of persons. They will do anything to get ahead.
5. The 'things of God' are second place to them, and
6. These people will enter the church and because of their lifestyles will ruin the church and its influence (see verse 17).

They are representing the church, and we should do all we can to not let them bring the church down—don't remain silent and allow them to cast a bad light on the church, ministry leaders or members. Ungodly work must not be condoned by silence or by taking a part in it!

So, there is such a thing as judging the consistently ungodly person who is ruining the church. This should be done without constantly *looking* for it or attacking anyone needlessly or in hatred! The love of God must always prevail in all things.

In 1 Corinthians 5:1-5, apostle Paul condemned the Corinthian church for remaining silent concerning a gross act of immorality in that church. He warned that this spoils the entire church if left unattended to. This is one of the passages where the church is commanded to deal with an evil act of immorality reference to fornication. They were reprimanded for not dealing with this problem. Compromising is *not* the way! Godliness is the way!

The Followers of Christ

Day 76

THE IMPORTANCE OF CONSTANT PRAYER

Psalm 27:11
> *Teach me how to live, O LORD. Lead me along the right path, for my enemies are waiting for me. (NLT)*

Psalm 27:11
> *Teach me thy way, O LORD, and lead me in a plain path, because of mine enemies. (KJV)*

There must be consistent prayer for the Lord to teach you how to live—to teach His way to His followers. Praying daily is vitally important for the spiritual growth and development of a follower of Jesus. Constant communion with the Lord will give direction and guidance into your life daily. Living like Jesus requires us to be constantly in prayer with humbleness of heart and faith in the Lord that He will lead and guide us throughout our day. The Lord will direct believers to live a quality life of commitment and dedication. He will also keep our enemies at bay.

The psalmist prayed to the Lord to teach him His ways. He was saying that he welcomed the Lord's guidance and direction in his life. David prayed, "Teach me, Lord." This was the earnest plea of a person who was humble enough to realize that God's perfection and excellence and wisdom was superior to his own. The psalmist acknowledged that God's wisdom exceeds his own! We should also approach God in the spirit of humbleness and total dependence on Him. As people of God and ministry leaders facing life's demands at home, in the community, in the church and at work, we should be aware of the need for the Lord to teach us how to live like Him. As we spend time with God in prayer, seek the Father's perspective on life, rather than coming to God with our own preconceived solutions and agenda. We must ask Him to teach us His ways, and then listen for His reply. Be ready to live according to His guidance. Is this your prayer today?

Day 77

JESUS IS A LOVE SONG

There are different types of love according to Scripture:

Eros = intimate love relationship between a man and a woman;

Phileo = friendship between family, friends, community, etc;

Agape = the Love of God for us and us for Him.

Jesus Christ commands us to *love*—to love God and our fellowman. This is a Portrait of Christ—Perfect Love personified in Jesus Christ. Jesus loves us unconditionally, whether sinner or not. This means that He loves all people, but do not love what a sinner does. That is why men, when they comes to Jesus can *still* receive forgiveness and salvation through the Blood of Jesus. He still loves us in spite of ourselves. In fact, Jesus is the example of *perfect* love. Romans 5:8 states, "But God commends His love toward us, in that, while we were yet sinners, Christ died for us" (KJV). He also said, "For God so loved the world that He gave His only begotten Son, that whosoever believes in Him shall not perish but have everlasting life" (KJV). It is said that love is a two way street. Love should be reciprocated. It would be wonderful if everyone would love Jesus the way He loves us. Mutual respect should be evident between man and God. Mutual respect and love should be shared between people also.

When people asked Jesus about the greatest of all commandments, he answered without hesitation that the two greatest commandments had to do with love—to love the One True God and another to *love* God's *imperfect* people. Is that hard? Yes, it certainly can be hard for us, but *not* for God! That is why we need God's Spirit in our hearts to love like we should. Otherwise, it is hard to love in many cases, because some people are not very lovable.

There are all kinds of people that we come across, some we like a lot, others we can tolerate, while others we can't stand at all. Love could also simply be shown as mutual respect for one another; it's like a contract to not do harm to your fellow man. Reality is that some people, even in the church world, we don't have the occasion to associate with, except to worship together. We spend more time with family and friends than with others, therefore; that love maybe deeper than with casual acquaintances. Remember, Jesus had 'beloved disciples' who He called upon to be *with* Him in prayer, and His inner circle; The Twelve, was with Him at *all* times in ministry.

In many (if not most) languages there is a clear distinction between liking someone versus loving someone. It is often said that God did not command us to like people, but to love them! Now, that may not make a whole lot of sense. Maybe a better way to say that is people should respect one another at the very least, whether we know them or not. We must have a love for all people, just like Christ. There is no distinction in Hebrew between "liking" and "loving"; the verb *le ahov* is one and the same for both. There is no difference; no varying levels of how to treat others.

Day 78

JESUS CHRIST SPELLS SUCCESS

David's success was opportunity received when presented to him by God. Our success can come by accepting opportunities presented to us by Christ. Christ is the key to our success! Opportunities received and acted upon equals blessings gained—total success!

David's success in his conquest/confrontation with Goliath brought him into the king's presence because he took advantage of an opportunity granted to him. Once there, Saul immediately wanted to find out more about the young man who had accomplished this great feat for Israel by defeating Goliath.

People of God need to assess all opportunities given them by God. What opportunities will come your way today as a result of the chance God gives you? You must discover how you can use your God given opportunities to honor others and God. When you take advantage of such opportunities, they will also result in blessings and success for you as well. The "doors of opportunity" will be opened to all of us with blessings and success!

1 Samuel 17:57-58
> *(57) And as David returned from the slaughter of the Philistine (Goliath), Abner took him, and brought him before Saul with the head of the Philistine in his hand. (58) And Saul said to him, whose son art thou, young man? And David answered. I am the son of thy servant Jesse the Bethlehemite. (KJV)*

David took advantage of his opportunity and we should accept our opportunities and receive our blessings!

Day 79

CHRIST, THE CHARACTER/IMAGE BUILDER

Proverbs 17:3
> *The refining pot is for silver and the furnace for gold, but the LORD tests the hearts. (NKJV)*

Jesus is a character builder. Testing and trials build character! The Lord tests the heart, mind, soul and spirit of man. Will you pass the test?

What does testing and trials look like for you? God uses adversity to transform our character to be more like Jesus. Today, when a challenge, a difficult person, or a forced change comes our way, we must take time to examine our response. It may be a moment of growth and development. Look at it as a means of growing and developing spiritually. God uses these moments to build our image. What does your response to adversity reveal? How does God want to transform you into the image of Christ through this experience? What can you do to give

Him greater access to your heart, head, hands, feet and habits? Christ is molding, melting, and making you to be like Him. It is only a test. Truly, the Lord tests our heart, mind, soul, and spirit for the purpose of building our image and character.

Day 80

JESUS PAID IT ALL

There is a hymn written by Grape and Hall that says, "Jesus paid it all, all to Him I owe. Sin had left a crimson stain—He washed it white as snow. I hear the Savior say, "Thy strength indeed is small! Child of weakness watch and pray, Find in me thine all in all."

John 3:16
"For God so loved the world that He gave His only begotten Son, that whoever believes in Him should not perish, but have everlasting life!" (NKJV)

Jesus perfected the plan of salvation for mankind that everyone may be saved. There is nothing that you have to pay to come to Jesus. Come without price. Come without money. The Lord bids you to come unto Him. This was an act of supreme love that He left His throne in glory to complete salvation's story. This is the ultimate act of love when a man gives up His life for His friends. Jesus paid the price for our salvation!

Day 81

LIFT JESUS UP

John 12:32
> *Jesus said, "And I, if I am lifted up from the earth, will draw all peoples to Myself." (NKJV)*

It is important to lift up the name of Jesus for the world to see and hear. Jesus Christ should be shown in our daily walk and in our conversation. Our lives should be a living testimony of the principles of Jesus by our life style. Satan's major tactic is to distract us from the things of God in order to promote his agenda. He will use the church to help him foster his plans. His job is to keep us from focusing on the things that are important to keeping the name of Jesus lifted up. He desires to see us debating about current issues and not promoting Jesus. He really wants to engage us in discussions that are controversial that are aimed at diluting the Word of God, and even suggesting that God's way of dealing with the world is different now. He wants us to debate the church, the Bible, salvation, Jesus and God. These things will result in talking about Jesus less and spending more time entertaining the devil's agenda. Believers need to stay focused on the things of God. Lift up the name of Jesus at all times in all 'manner of conversation.'

Day 82

...OUR FAITH TO REMAIN STRONG

John 14:11-14

(11) Jesus said to His disciples, "Believe Me that I am in the Father, and the Father in Me; or else believe Me for the very works' sake. (12) Verily, verily, I say unto you, He that believeth on me, the works that I do shall he do also; and greater works than these shall he do; because I go unto my Father. (13) And whatsoever ye shall ask in my name, that will I do, that the Father may be glorified in the Son. (14) "If ye shall ask anything in My name, I will do it!" (KJV)

Jesus wants His followers to believe in Him and His Word. With a strong faith in God, we cannot be overtaken by Satan and his forces. If you believe in Christ, His word, and pray constantly, you will remain strong in faith. Jesus was teaching His disciples to believe that He and God the Father are one. There is unity in the Godhead—the Trinity. If there is a difficult problem in believing that, Jesus says, then believe in Me for the works that I have done—healing the sick, raising the dead, opening blind eyes, bringing salvation to the lost—the miracles that I performed in front of your eyes. Jesus further taught His disciples that greater works than I have done, you will do because I am going back to My Father. Jesus left His followers to be ambassadors for Him. He instilled a strong faith statement in them by saying, anything you ask in My name, I will do it! This should be the declaration of faith for all believers: Jesus will do it!

Day 83

THE SPHERE OF POSITIVE INFLUENCE

Colossians 1:15-17
*(15) The Son is the image of the invisible God, the firstborn over
all creation. (16) For in him all things were created: things in
heaven and on earth, visible and invisible, whether thrones or
powers or rulers or authorities; all things have been created
through him and for him. (17) He is before all things, and in
him all things hold together.*

These verses speak to the Supremacy of Jesus Christ as
the Son of God. He is one with God. Jesus influences
me. Jesus Christ is the image and likeness of God who is
invisible to us, but is personified in His Son Jesus Christ.
God has made all things, therefore; His Son Jesus Christ is
also included in the creation and since we can relate to
Him as the mediator between God and man, it can be said
that, He is the sphere of influence for the all believers. He
is our role model! Through Him, we should display the
Image of Christ in our lives as well.

The circle of positive influence is in that after Christ
has saved you, you can positively affect someone else.
Christ is then glorified! The Christian believer's sphere of
influence should also be evident in the world because we
have Christ on the inside of us. Our influence is not just
at the church setting, but it is everywhere we go.
Followers of Christ must be a positive influence on the
job, at school, in the community, in the marketplace, in the
home or at play. This is called lifestyle evangelism where
the believer lives according to the influence of Christ via
the Holy Spirit in our lives, then our lives should influence

others.

It should be very rewarding to have a positive influence on the people around sometimes without saying any words at all—just living the life. That is the way Christ uses His people to bring about change in the lives of people. Helping others will also bless us.

As the Creator and Lord of life, Jesus' life of servant-hood stretched from the synagogue leaders to His family, friends, beggars, strangers, tax collectors, and Roman officials. Jesus intends for you and I to influence the thinking, behavior, and development of every person who comes across our paths. This type of interchange will be a positive influence for the entire world around us. Be a positive influence to everyone you come in contact with in your daily life.

Day 84

JESUS IS PERFECT PEACE (SHALOM)

Jesus is the epitome of peace and tranquility. He is Shalom—Perfect Peace! *Shalom* is a Hebrew word meaning peace, completeness, prosperity, and welfare and can be used idiomatically to mean both hello and goodbye. Shalom can also refer to peace between two entities (for example, between an individual and God or between a group of individuals), or peace to the well-being, welfare, or safety of an individual (*Wikipedia*).

John 14:25-27
> *(25) "These things I have spoken to you while being present with you. (26) "But the Helper, the Holy Spirit, Whom the Father will send in My name, He will teach you all things, and bring to your remembrance all things that I said to you. (27) "Peace I leave with you, My Peace I give to you; not as the world gives do I give to you. Let not your heart be troubled, neither let it be afraid." (NKJV)*

Jesus is comforting His grieving disciples after they discovered that He would not be with them any longer in the earthly realm. But, He was letting them know that He would still be their peace as the Father was going to send them another comforter, in the name of Jesus! He wanted them to know that He would always be their peace, even though He was going away.

In Jesus we can also have perfect peace because we have Jesus Christ on the inside via the Holy Spirit (the executor of the Godhead). The Bible paints Jesus as the personification of peace in several passages of scripture throughout the written Word, and through the testimonies and witness of men and women throughout the ages. We must never forget that in a world of deep confusion and turmoil, in Christ we have peace. He is our Peace! Christ is the answer for the world today. He will abide with you. He will live in you. Christ will take abode in your heart through the Holy Spirit and commune with you. He will comfort you and give you peace—He will grant you perfect peace—Shalom!

God's word is our assurance in that the Word of God even states in Isaiah 26:3-4:

(3) You will keep him in Perfect Peace whose mind is stayed on You, because he trusts in You. (4) Trust in the Lord forever, for in Yah, the Lord, is everlasting strength. (NKJV)

And another assurance is in John 16:33:

"These things I have spoken to you, that in Me you may have peace. In the world you will have tribulation; but be of good cheer, I have overcome the world." (NKJV)

What marvelous assurances of the Perfect Peace of Christ we have through Jesus Christ our Lord!

Day 85

CHRIST: THE CHANGE AGENT
HOW OPEN ARE YOU TO CHANGE?

All of us have a tendency to want to control or protect certain aspects of our lives. God, however; wants free access to every part of us—motivations, thoughts, relationships, behaviors, daily practices. As God, He has the right to step in and rearrange our plans, goals, priorities, and dreams at any time. When He does, it is for our benefit, growth, and development. As believers, keep in mind that we are obligated by God to 'grow in grace' daily. God doesn't want any stagnant Christians. He wants believers who are dynamic and moving forward. We must allow God to take control of our lives to bring about positive change. God can always be trusted to do the right thing for us. He will not steer you wrong. God is constantly calling us to progress and to move forward. He is calling us to become closer to the likeness and image of His Son, Jesus Christ. We should not be afraid for Him to take our hands and lead us. We must trust Him with our life to mold us into what He will have us to be. We are His workmanship.

The hymn writer, John S. Norris and E. W. Blandy penned the words to "Where He Leads Me." "I can hear my Savior calling, I can hear my Savior calling, I can hear my Savior calling, Take thy cross and follow, follow Me." "Where He leads me I will follow, Where He leads me I will follow, Where He leads me I will follow—I'll go with Him, with Him all the way." Yes, all the way with Jesus Christ! Where is He calling you to trustingly follow Him today? Changes will come in life—some good and some bad, but Christ can use any of our circumstances to cause us to *grow* spiritually. Will you be ready to go with God wherever He leads?

Matthew 9:9
> *As Jesus went on from there, he saw a man named Matthew sitting at the tax collector's booth. "Follow me," he told him, and Matthew got up and followed him.*

Matthew followed Christ willingly and without question. He trustingly followed Jesus and his life would never be the same anymore.

Day 86

LOVE BY SUPREME SACRIFICE

Ephesians 2:4-5
> *(4) But God, who is rich in mercy, for his great love wherewith he loved us, (5) even when we were dead in sins, hath quickened us together with Christ, (by grace ye are saved). (KJV)*

You are supremely loved by God. Jesus' death and resurrection is an act of God's supreme love for us all (see John 3:16). We are no longer dead to sin but alive; no longer blinded by pride and sin but humbly aware of whose we are in Christ; no longer are we immobilized by guilt and fear but forgiven and confident in the power of His Spirit. Let His love and life transform your life. Let His grace have its full effect in your life and Christian experience.

Day 87

JESUS, THE PERSONIFICATION OF GOD THE FATHER

John 14:8-10

(8) Phillip said unto Jesus, "Lord, show us the Father, and it is sufficient for us." Then Jesus replied, (9) "Have I been with you so long, and yet you have not known Me, Phillip? He who has seen Me (Christ) has seen the Father; so how can you say, 'Show us the Father'? (10)"Do you not believe that I am in the Father, and the Father in Me?" The words that I speak to you I do not speak on My own authority; but the Father who dwells in Me does the works." (NKJV)

If you have received Jesus Christ as your personal Savior, you also have received the Father. For those who say 'there is no God,' they have not by faith received the Son of God. Jesus is the personification of God. We must receive Christ within our hearts in faith and at the same time, we also receive the Father for the Father and the Son are one. Jesus made this message very clear to His disciples. He wanted them to know that He was and is the divine Son of God, the second person of the Godhead who is in the image of God. They are in unity and harmony. In knowing Jesus, you also know the Father and have seen Him! Further, you being a child of God are made to be in the likeness and image of Jesus Christ because He is in you! How do we know there is a God? Because we know Jesus!

Day 88

JESUS CHRIST KNOWS EVERYTHING ABOUT US

Jesus Christ is omniscient just like the Father. He knows everything about you. You should never fear anything because Christ knows even before you ask what you have need of. Often people fear changes that occur in their lives, but Jesus is aware of them also. Scripture states, for whom he did foreknow, he also did predestinate to be conformed to the image of his Son, that he might be the firstborn among many brethren (Rom 8:29, KJV).

Christ was born first, and will be followed by many others, who will be His brothers. That includes you and me! If we are conformed to the image of Christ, how can we be anything except what Jesus Christ is—especially in the light of when we consider the New Testament emphasis for His followers to change to be as He is—Paul states in Ephesians 4:13 that we are to grow to the measure of the stature of the fullness of Christ. This more than implies a period of spiritual growth and development or maturity to become like Christ.

Therefore, Jesus is aware of all of our needs even before we were born and before we ask. The changes that occur in our lives happen to shape us, melt us, make us, and mold us into what He wants us to be. He desires that we be in the image of God's Son. Changes may come and cause discomfort and frustrations, but God is taking us through various stages of transformation to make us better and to make us more like Jesus. Changes are difficult to face and to handle—and life is full of them. Sometimes we resist change, hate change, or we may embrace change. Those are the choices. We must know that Christ knows everything about us and will not steer us in the wrong direction—no matter what comes or goes—He uses change to develop or mature us. What will you choose today? Don't be afraid of change, because God just may be molding you into the image of Jesus Christ! Just like seasons change, we change, and God through Christ knows the affects!

From the time we are born until we die, we are involved in constant change. We arrive in this world as babies with everything in our body that we need to live, survive and thrive. If we are fortunate enough to be healthy, our bodies continue to change as we grow into children, teens, young adults, median adults and senior adults. Our personalities develop; our education and life experiences continue to formulate who we are and how we interact with the world around us.

Change is always around us as well. The earth passes through seasons every year. Plants, trees and flowers come alive, live and give us joy and then die away or become dormant to live again next year. It's an amazing process and one in which we are often unaware.

Once we become followers of Jesus, change continues all around us as God's plan is to conform (or change) us into the likeness of His Son (Rom 8:29). The maturation process is sometimes slow, sometimes difficult but always with us. As we read the Scriptures, new ways to change are revealed to us and we change again and again, sometimes with joy and gladness and sometimes with pain and tears.

How has God changed you? In what ways is He

molding you into the person who is conformed to the image of Christ? What have you read in Scripture recently that the Holy Spirit has challenged you to grow in – to change? Are you willing to enter the journey with joy or are you dreading the process? Will you commit to an image or portrait of Christ today?

Day 89

WHAT WILL YOU GIVE?

Philippians 2:5-8
> *(5) In your relationships with one another, have the same mindset Christ Jesus: (6) Who, being in very nature God, did not consider equality with God something to be grasped, but made himself nothing, (7) taking the very nature of a servant, being made in human likeness. (8) And being found in appearance as a man, he humbled himself and became obedient to death—even death on a cross!*

Jesus counted the cost and determined that we were worth the cost. The above verse gives one of the strongest assertions in the New Testament of the deity of Jesus Christ. The Greek word *morphe* is translated as He has the very nature of God the Father. This is very significant! All of the attributes in God are in Jesus as well! He came to earth in human form possessing the very nature of God. This is a testament to the meekness and self-humbling of Christ and Paul said our attitude should be the same as that of Jesus Christ—humility. Because of the humility of Christ, God exalted Him to the highest place and gave Him the name that is above every name that at the sound of that name every knee must bow and every tongue must confess that Jesus Christ is Lord to the glory of God. So, just like Jesus humbled Himself, we must be humble servants of the Lord.

Jesus paid it all—suffering, humiliation, pain, and death. He paid the ultimate cost so we can give Him our life and testimony and worship.

Jesus counted up the cost of redeeming humankind and determined that it was worth it all. The whole plan of salvation history—creation, incarnation, persecution, suffering, death—was all worth it. We were worth the price of Jesus' crucifixion and sacrifice! Jesus came as a humble servant. Now, we must follow in His footsteps as one of His disciples. The cost for our discipleship is to follow Christ! Give Him our life! That is the cost for us! Are you willing to follow Him today?

Day 90

EVENTS LEADING UP TO THE CRUCIFIXION AND RESURRECTION OF JESUS

Think on these things: the events leading up to the crucifixion and resurrection of Jesus Christ that can be a lesson for us in our lifestyle as a Christian.

1. He was betrayed by His disciple Judas. One of His trusted disciples became His enemy for monetary gain. Judas sold Jesus out for a measly 30 pieces of silver—maybe less than a thousand dollars in today's money. Jesus being in human form like we are and

probably felt deep sorrow in being let down by one of His own people. Can you imagine being betrayed by a friend, family member or marriage partner? Therefore, the pain that Jesus felt physically was also an emotional experience that can hurt very deeply to the core of the heart. Many of us today have let Jesus down in many ways just to benefit our own selfish interests and desires. Let us not be selfish in our living the life of a Christian representing Jesus Christ. Remember, Jesus gave His life and forgave us when we didn't deserve it.

2.	He rode into the streets of Jerusalem on the back of a donkey as the "Triumphant Savior." This event is celebrated in modern times as The Triumphant Entry of Jesus commonly called *Palm Sunday*—the Sunday before Easter when Jesus' resurrection is celebrated. The events starting with Palm Sunday is called Holy Week where Jesus certifies Himself as King. For the first time, Jesus publicly acknowledged that He is the Messiah. The people followed along crying out "Hosanna" to the King of Kings. In the days that followed, they abandoned Him. When the moment came for them to speak up for Jesus, they cried out, "Crucify Him!" The lesson in this is that you must be careful of who lauds you now, because in the end, those same people may turn their backs on you. Even more, you must be mindful yourself not to be hypocritical about your response to Jesus Christ and your response to your fellow man. Stick with Christ at all times.

3.	Peter denied Christ, but all of His other disciples also ran and denied knowing the Lord because of deep fear for their lives. People often deny knowing Christ today by the lives they live and by the shame and embarrassment that they feel in the midst of their friends. Scripture states that all of Jesus' disciples—the inner circle fled in fear after Jesus' arrest (see Mark 14:50). Jesus was left to suffer and die alone being abandoned by His disciples who knew and He had done no wrong. We can say now, 'what a shame,' but many people do that today as well. Let us not be afraid to worship and serve the Lord Jesus anywhere or anytime. The followers of Satan are bold about doing Satan's work. Bold about doing and being true followers of Jesus Christ today.

4.   It is recorded that Jesus agonized so intensely in those moments leading up to His crucifixion that He sweat drops of blood (Lk 22:44). He was in deep prayer to God, but felt the emotional pain of the impending suffering that He would face. Jesus' terrible plight started while He was in prayer and was thinking about what He had to face. Don't think for a moment that Jesus does not know how you feel when faced with adversity. He knows! He also cares! You should appreciate what Christ did for you and worship and praise Him at all times.

5.   He was falsely accused and rejected by Jewish religious leaders. Can you imagine the heartache Jesus experienced when the very people He was sent to save spat in His face, blindfolded Him, cursed Him and accused Him of blasphemy? The Sanhedrin Council set up a "kangaroo court" and sentenced the Son of God to death. He had done no wrong! It is like today when the very place where you seek covering is the very place where you receive betrayal and a lack of sensitivity to

your problems. Some of the worse hurt in the world is the hurt you encounter by the church or your family. Christ was betrayed by His own people. Lesson for us to learn is that Jesus will never let us down. He will never betray us like man, so we must not betray Him. Jesus did not open His mouth in self-defense when He was falsely accused. Now, when Satan accuses us, Jesus argues our case and declares us not guilty! Jesus stands in for us in all situations.

6.   He was mocked and abused by Roman guards. After Pilate caved under pressure from the Jews, Roman soldiers flogged Jesus with a whip, drove a crown of thorns into His scalp, beat His head with sticks and mockingly pretended to worship Him. The flogging alone—which would have involved leather cords with pieces of lead or bone attached—would have drained much of Jesus' blood. What a cruel thing to do to our Lord and Savior. Jesus could have rejected this punishment, but He chose to endure the pain because He loved His people so much. He was on a mission for humanity and it had to be fulfilled.

7.   He was crucified between two thieves in a public show of embarrassment. It is difficult to imagine the excruciating pain that Jesus suffered during the act of crucifixion. Metal spikes were driven into Jesus' hands and feet, and He had to slide His mangled body up against the wood of the cross in order to catch His breath. I understand that the spikes were around nine inches long. And because it was the habit of Romans to crucify criminals naked, Jesus endured the ultimate shame and humiliation by being naked. Most people don't really think about this fact that people who are

crucified are naked—maximum humiliation. What's more, He hung on that crude cross next to two men who had been convicted of crimes, while He was completely innocent. Jesus died in the place of *all* of *humanity*. Jesus took our place on the cross!

8.   His body was pierced with a spear. Even after Jesus took His last breath, a soldier jabbed a spear up through the chest cavity—most likely to make sure Jesus was dead. John tells us that blood and water spilled out (John 19:34). Just as Adam's side was opened to bring forth the first woman, Jesus' side was opened to bring forth the church. His piercing produced a fountain of life for us.

9.   He experienced death for the whole world. The horrible way that He died was the way that the Romans crucified criminals. Was Jesus a criminal? Was He guilty of any crime whatsoever? Did He do anything wrong? The resounding answer is *no*. He did nothing wrong and was not guilty of any crime. He only loved people and fulfilled the promise of the Lord God that He would leave His home in glory and come down to save sinners like us. His love was supreme. He loved us while we were yet sinners. Now, that is real love. The good news of the whole matter is that He did not stay in the grave. He got up! He got the victory in it all, and because of that He provided a way for everyone to be saved. He tasted death and the grave and is sensitive to our needs as well. Therefore, we should never fear anything that is going on in our life, because Jesus already is aware of what we are facing. Have faith in Him.

10.   Jesus was resurrected with all power is His hand.

Therefore, His people also have the victory! We are victorious!

Day 91

A GRATEFUL HEART RESPONDS TO A GIVING SAVIOR

A grateful heart praises God for the blessing of salvation and life. Many times, the spiritual gifts and blessings given to us are often for our own edification only. Spreading that testimony may not be intended for anyone else. However, there may come a time when that testimony and blessing of the Lord may be shared with others.

Jesus' compassion often is evident in His response to mankind. In the Bible, He was found displaying His compassion time after time to those who were in need of spiritual and physical miracles and blessings. On one occasion, He compassionately responded to a man with leprosy, healed him, and gave him his life back. He does the same thing for us and gives us life. A grateful heart also means obedience to Jesus Christ. We must live in obedience to Christ! This man in the focal verse did not obey the command of Jesus. Jesus had told him not to tell anyone. I can understand his happiness and motivation to tell of his blessing of healing, but Jesus had told him not to tell it now. Will you obey the commands of Jesus today? What is Jesus telling you today? Do we not hear Jesus speaking to us? What interferes with your obedience to Christ today?

Mark 1:45

Instead he went out and began to talk freely, spreading the news. As a result, Jesus could no longer enter a town openly but stayed outside in lonely places. Yet the people still came to him from everywhere.

The grateful man was excited and happy about his healing and did not follow the command of Christ to tell no one about this miracle at this time. Instead, he spread the news. Even though this didn't seem to be a bad thing, he still disobeyed Jesus and it caused Him not to be able to enter a town without being flooded with people following Him before He was ready.

Obedience is an important element in this miracle account. Even with the man's gratefulness for his miracle, he still failed to obey Christ to not spread the news. He should have simply enjoyed his blessing himself and be edified by it himself! A time may come to testify. Until then just be grateful yourself.

Day 92

ON DESPERATELY SEEKING JESUS CHRIST

In Mark 2, we find Jesus teaching crowds, people who came, observing, hoping to be amazed by Him, and they are not disappointed. The critics, teachers of the law, taking notes, wait to pounce on anything that doesn't align with their thinking; they, too, are not disappointed. Then came some men desperately seeking Jesus, one paralyzed others willing to do anything to get their friend to Jesus. These are the ones who are transformed; they, too, are not disappointed, but find all that Jesus has to offer. Are you desperately seeking Jesus for something today?

Mark 2:9-11

(9) "Which is easier: to say to this paralyzed man, 'Your sins are forgiven,' or to say, 'Get up, take your mat and walk'? (10) But I want you to know that the Son of Man has authority on earth to forgive sins." So he said to the man, (11) "I tell you, get up, take your mat and go home."

Out of everything that we need as a people physically, there is nothing more important than having our spiritual needs met. It is absolutely necessary that a man has his soul set free and nourished. Our emotional, spiritual, and internal needs have to be satisfied, even more so than our physical bodies. If a man doesn't have comfort and peace of heart, mind, soul, and spirit met, he is like 'the walking dead.' That is why it is so important to worship God in Spirit and truth. Then his soul can be sufficiently nourished.

When there are human needs, Jesus is always ready to minister to our needs. Jesus provides the answer for all of our needs: physical, spiritual, emotional. It is wonderful to have a Savior who can provide for us in every way. He moves by the Holy Spirit. All we have to do is depend on Him by faith. How many of us are hungry for God? How many of us are thirsty for God? How many of us are lost without God? He is the air we breathe. He is our daily bread. Cry out to the Lord Jesus daily if you want more of Him. Seek for more of Him and for the floodgates of blessings to open. This should be our quest primarily! We should "desperately seek after God!" The song I share here with you speaks to our prayer for God to fill our hearts, acknowledging that He is the very substance and sustenance that we need for our life.

This is the air I breathe
This is the air I breathe
Your Holy presence living in me
This is my daily bread
This is my daily bread
Your very word spoken to me
And I, I'm desperate for You
And I, I'm lost without You
And I, I'm desperate for You
And I, I'm lost without You
I'm lost without You
I'm lost without You
I'm desperate for You

(Songwriters: Flint, Keith Charles / Howlett, Liam / Palmer, Keith Andrew Published by: Lyrics © Kobalt Music Publishing Ltd., Universal Music Publishing Group, Warner/Chappell Music, Inc., EMI Music Publishing)

Day 93

WHAT CONDITION IS YOUR SOUL IN TODAY?

How is your soul? How would you answer that question today? Are you stressed, carrying the weight of your responsibilities, wondering which way to go? The state of a believer's soul matters. Just as Jesus took time to tend to the state of His soul, He urges us to make our relationship with God our number one priority. The state of our soul is crucial to how we interact with others—and how we care about ourselves. How is your soul today?

Believers tend to the soul by constantly staying in contact with God through prayer and fasting; praise and worship; communion and communication with God; fellowshipping with the godly. By doing this, God will refresh our souls daily. We *must* guard our hearts and souls.

Matthew 22:36-40
> *(36) "Teacher, which is the greatest commandment in the Law?" (37) Jesus replied: "'Love the Lord your God with all your heart and with all your soul and with all your mind.' (38) This is the first and greatest commandment. (39) And the second is like it: 'Love your nighbor as yourself.' (40) All the Law and the Prophets hang on these two commandments."*

Check the status of your soul to see what kind of condition it may be in today. Give your total self to Jesus and He will comfort your soul, heart, mind, and spirit. He will calm the turbulent waters of your soul and still the storms from deep within. He will give us the desires of our heart!

Day 94

SEEK AFTER GOD THROUGH JESUS CHRIST

Nations and individuals who live life without God and keeping His commandments will utterly fall. The following is both a historical and prophetic word.

Leviticus 18:26-28
> *(26) But you must keep my decrees and my laws. The native-born and the foreigners residing among you must not do any of these detestable things, (27) for all these things were done by the people who lived in the land before you, and the land became defiled. (28) And if you defile the land, it will vomit you out as it vomited out the nations that were before you.*

Because of man's lawlessness, this law of the universe has too often gone into effect, even true today! As a law of an impartial God, it will soon descend upon the nations of Israel in the form of "a nation of fierce countenance" (Deut 28:49-50). It is only a matter of time—so says the Bible concerning Israel.

In history, the Roman Empire fell; the third Reich fell; Jerusalem fell; Judea fell; the Babylonian Empire; and several nations of today all fell. One thing for sure an unrighteous nation or individual will suffer this plight if they don't seek after God and respect His authority. Godlessness breeds degradation and utter destruction. It is only a matter of time when other nations may fall. The move towards secularization is already in motion and it is detrimental! Not good! A Godless nation is a dying nation!

Proverbs 14:34 says, "Righteousness exalts a nation, but sin *is* a reproach to *any* people" (NKJV). When a nation descends into perversions like homosexuality and same-sex "marriage," its decline accelerates, its moral fibers weaken, and it becomes ripe for disaster, either naturally, politically, or militarily. If the leadership of a nation participates in these perversions, the immorality spreads like a cancer among the people, accelerating the collapse of the nation and the individual. The leaders, already perverted personally, make immoral and unwise decisions regarding the nation's direction and conditions grow worse (see Rom 1:26-32; 2 Tim 3:13). Knowing the nation's destruction may be ever so near, Christians have a responsibility to pray and seek God's face. Let us pray for ourselves, our country and all nations of the world.

Day 95

JESUS, THE COMPASSIONATE SAVIOR

Mark 6:34
> *And Jesus, when He came out, saw a great multitude and was moved with compassion for them, because they were like sheep not having a shepherd. So He began to teach them many things. (NKJV)*

When Jesus saw the needs of the people, He was moved with compassion. Jesus is a compassionate Savior today also. He sees the needs of people and ministers to those needs through His Spirit and through His servants. Jesus was always ready to show compassion to those who crossed His path. Even though He was tired, He still ministered to those who were in need of a shepherd. Jesus will also have compassion on us. Isn't it reassuring to know that Jesus is always ready to minister to our needs? He understands our need for shepherding.

The simplicity of being like Jesus focuses on our ability to touch and affect the lives of those around us. As followers of Christ, we should influence positive changes in the lives of those who we come in contact with. Living, loving and leading like Jesus doesn't require a complex set of rules, but just a heart of compassion like Jesus. This means that we must have an awareness of the needs of those persons who we are around on a daily basis using our skills, talents, resources and abilities to meet their needs. There must be a willingness to serve, to help, to assist in the growth and development of those who are in need of our help. This is what it means to be a portrait of Christ—an image of Christ. Will you become more aware of the people around you today?

Day 96

FORGIVENESS: LIVING IN THE IMAGE OF CHRIST

1 John 1:8-10
> *(8) "If we claim we have no sin, we are only fooling ourselves and not living in the truth. (9) But if we confess our sins to him, he is faithful and just to forgive us our sins and to cleanse us from all wickedness. (10) If we claim we have not sinned, we are calling God a liar and showing that his word has no place in our hearts." (NLT)*

Admitting you were wrong simply requires you saying: "I'm sorry!" Why is it *so* difficult for people to say, "I'm sorry" or admit that they were wrong? Many times, if they are sorry, they simply won't say it, but instead just go on as if nothing happened. This is one of the most hurting things, especially among church folk. All of us have had opportunities to admit that we've been wrong—a careless word, a thoughtless action, a missed opportunity, a self-serving act; they just happen. But, the fact is not too many people will let a person know that they are sorry. I have made it a point to tell my kids "I'm sorry" whenever I got them wrong even from a very young age. I would always say, 'I'm sorry.' This teaches honesty and integrity to a child. None of us are right all the time. When we are wrong simply say I am sorry.

This can also have carryover value in asking God for forgiveness for doing wrong. Admit it and ask God to forgive you. Some church members and ministry leaders alike simply will not do it! Apostle John whom Jesus loved gives us an action plan to follow when we do not live, love, or lead like Jesus. Allow God to redeem your failures, like He did those of the first disciples. Ask God for forgiveness for your sins and failures and allow His redeeming power to prevail! This attitude will keep Christ's disciples in the right channel to live in the image of Christ.

Day 97

'TO BE LIKE JESUS...' OH HOW I WANT TO BE LIKE HIM

Galatians 2:8
> *For the same God who worked through Peter as the apostle to the Jews also worked through me as the apostle to the Gentiles.*
> *(NLT)*

It's all about Jesus Christ. The same God who worked through Peter, Paul, and the others will work through us also. What Jesus was about, we should also be about. What Jesus did, we should also do. He did say "greater things we will do."

Allow God to shine through you today! Lift Jesus up through your lifestyle! God has given each of us an arena of life—a sphere of influence—in which He calls us to serve others on a daily basis. To be a servant of Jesus Christ should be a major goal of every follower of Christ. God places us all in unique places to witness for Christ at home, at work, in church, in the community or wherever we may be. We should be aware of where God has placed us each day to be an example of the love of Jesus. Someone is always looking at us which gives us a chance to 'let our light shine' so that someone may experience the love of Jesus through us. It may be by our children and the examples that we display in how we deal with people and life. It may be fellow employees on the job who are looking at us as someone who wholeheartedly follows and emulates Jesus on a daily basis. People may be looking at us without our noticing it. They may be consciously or unconsciously modeling their life after ours. Let it be worthy of our witness of Jesus. Let God shine through you today.

Matthew 5:13-16 (The Beatitudes from the Sermon on the Mount)
(13) "You are the salt of the earth, but if the salt loses its flavor, how shall it be seasoned? It is then good for nothing but to be thrown out and trampled underfoot by men. (14) "You are the light of the world a city that is set on a hill cannot be hidden. (15) "Nor do they light a lamp and put it under a basket, but on a lamp-stand, and it gives light to all who are in the house. (16) "Let your light so shine before men, that they may see your good works and glorify your Father in heaven." (NKJV)

Day 98

CHRIST IS OUR SUPREME EXAMPLE

Which way should we go today? Whatever we do, let it be guided by Jesus Christ. Live your daily life by the standards and values of Jesus Christ.

John 12:26
Whoever serves me must follow me; and where I am, my servant also will be. My Father will honor the one who serves Me.

Life is so full of ups and downs. Sometimes, we just don't know which way to go. Life has so many twists and turns—hills and valleys. Sometimes, it is very difficult to traverse. One consoling fact is that when we live our lives in the will of God, He will see us through the difficult moments. Jesus Christ came to earth in the likeness of sinful flesh to give us an example of how to depend on God for the answers to solving the problems of life. We don't know every path to take on a daily basis, but God knows. Christ is our Supreme example as to how to live life. When difficult problems occur and difficult decisions have to be made, Jesus will be with us to help us take the right paths. This is reassuring! Look to Jesus!

The secret to living life is in following Jesus, because Jesus says that wherever He is, His servants will also be. The Scripture says that whoever serves Jesus honors the Father and the Father will honor the servant of the Lord.

How would your life be different today if you were making conscious choices and decisions to live your life according to good moral values? It starts with Jesus Christ! You can say that something is important to you, but your words and actions reveal what is in your heart and head. Taking time to reflect on and reaffirm your values and standards, including your commitment to live, love, and be like Jesus, solidifies and intensifies your motivation to do just that. How will you live differently today as a servant of the Lord Jesus? Follow Christ in realness!

Day 99

FAITH IN GOD PLEASES HIM BEYOND MEASURE

Hebrews 11:1
> *Faith is the substance of things hoped for, the evidence of things not seen. (NKJV)*

This verse really has reference to a basic, fundamental belief in God. Many times it is associated with faith in receiving things that are hoped for, but before receiving anything from God, one must first believe in God Himself. A genuine belief in God will result in believing God for anything whatsoever. Faith in God pleases Him to the utmost! The Bible also says: "But without faith it is impossible to please Him, for he who comes to God must believe that He is a rewarder of those who diligently seek Him" (Heb 11:6, NKJV).

After discussing the comparisons between Judaism and God's principles in the first ten chapters, the author of Hebrews changes the discussion in chapter eleven to charging the Hebrews to hold on to their new found faith and not to shrink back. The writer encouraged them to look at all the soldiers who had gone on before and fought a good fight of faith. The exhortation was for them to be firm in their faith in God. Also for us today, we must also have a firm belief in God as the foundation for our faith. The scripture affirms that without faith, it is impossible to please God, not so much for things, but for God Himself. God is a jealous God, and nothing should be placed before Him! It pleases God for us to respect and honor Him.

Seek God diligently and persevere in faith in order to accomplish the tasks that are presented. Faith is the key. Let us believe God today without doubt!

Day 100

JESUS IS OUR MORAL COMPASS

John 5:24
> *"I tell you the truth, whoever hears my word and believes him who sent me has eternal life and will not be condemned (for their sins); he has crossed over from death to life."*

Jesus Christ is our moral compass by which we define how to live our lives. Real living occurs when we give our lives completely to Jesus. The Scripture declares that when we receive Him, we pass from death to life. Our daily existence will be determined by Jesus. He is the one who points us in the direction which we should go. When we try to do it on our own, there is the possibility of errors and misdirection. The way to ensure that we are going in the right direction is to allow Jesus to lead and guide our footsteps.

Life is full of ups and downs. Sometimes, it is difficult for us to find our way amid all of the chaos in the world. But Jesus will lead and guide so that there will be no missteps along the way. After all, life is not always simple and "cut and dry," but it can be very challenging. With Jesus determining the direction that we should go, then the journey will be much easier. After all, there is more to life than simple pleasures and easy rules to follow. With Christ in our heart, we have the directing force in our life. He moves within us by His Spirit.

Whether we admit or not, all of us desire to live life to the fullest, and if at all possible to live life problem free, mistake free, and full of success. No one wants negative experiences to occur in their life. The reality of life is that there are good and bad experiences—good and bad days that we must face, with Christ, we can face them with strength and courage.

Jesus demonstrated that there is more to life and being human than what the world offers. We must follow His example! When we are willing to trust God's heart, God's truth, and God's way, we will discover life as God intended it to be. We find abundant life not so much by asserting ourselves, but through humble trust in Jesus Christ. The life that Jesus offers is a life full of possibilities and positive direction. Christ offers *abundant life*! John 10:10-11 says, "The thief does not come except to steal, and to kill, and to destroy. I have come that they may have life, and that they may have it more abundantly. I (Jesus Christ) am the good shepherd. The good shepherd gives His life for the sheep" (NKJV). Jesus is our moral compass and our way to a beautiful life. Have you found the life Jesus offers today?

Day 101

SEEK JESUS CHRIST AND NOT EVIL

Isaiah 55:6-7
(6) Seek the LORD while he may be found; call on him while he is near. (7) Let the wicked forsake his way and the evil (or unrighteous) man his thoughts; Let him return to the LORD, and he will have mercy on him; and to our God, for he will abundantly (or freely) pardon. (NKJV)

The very wording in this exhortation implies that Israel did exactly what He did not want them to do. They sought satisfaction and fulfillment in the world—things that do not satisfy. They did not trust the Lord God completely. They believed the world's perspective and practiced it, thus rejecting God and His Word. The lesson for today is to abide in the precepts of God and practice His way. There may come a time where it may be difficult to find Him, therefore; seek Him now. That is a wise decision. Seek the Lord while He may be found!

There is a tremendous blessing in seeking Christ—we can have abundant life now and eternal life in that day when He comes to 'make up His jewels.' As He declared in His word, they shall be mine! Seeking after evil is detrimental to our spiritual and physical well-being. It will spell death to us in every way. Seeking after Christ means life, blessings, and success. It is good to belong to Christ!

Day 102

THOUGHTS ON THE RELIGIOUS LIFE IN CHRIST

Never forget that as a believer—a Christian—that Christ is our Lord, Savior, Deliverer, and Redeemer. That is the bottom line in living life as a believer in Christ. Follower of Christ, live your life in Him. Apostle John wrote the words of Christ, "And I, if I be lifted up from the earth, will draw all men unto me (12:32, KJV).

I have always tried to live for the Lord, ever since I was a teenager. I *am* human, but I endeavored to be one who would try to be an example of what he preached, sang, and testified about. It may not have been easy *all* the time, but I was always determined not to be like what I saw around me from people and preachers all over the area where I'm from who pretended to be holy! I hear several young people today asking the question: "Is there anyone trying to live according to the dictates of the Bible?" No wonder so many people think it's alright to do any and everything; they have been convinced that being human, God understands and He always forgives. Yes He does, but it's no excuse for trivializing the church, the Bible, or God Himself! God created us in His image and likeness, therefore; we are His moral agents! God created us to live our lives like Him.

Jesus is our intercessor between God and man. In Jesus, we can relate to what it means to be like God because Jesus came to earth in the likeness of sinful flesh. He experienced what it is like to be in human flesh and still trust in God for life. By the Holy Spirit, man can receive that part of God that ministers to our spirit man. This is where we can receive ministry to our spirits and, thus; live for God.

Through the Holy Spirit who resides within us, live the life you sing, preach, teach, and testify about. No pretending! This is not to say that any human is perfect—but I do believe that the believer should be progressing towards perfection. Salvation and perfection is progressive. A Christian serious about his or her walk goes through a process of sanctification. The life we live should speak loudly in 'lifting up the name of Jesus,' even without saying a word.

Jesus Christ is our ultimate role model and example for life. He is our major example (our chief cornerstone). We must always look to Jesus as the pattern for our lives, the author and finisher of our faith! The old song of the church says, "To be like Jesus, O how I want to be like Him!" Really, He wants it this way, and I *do* believe there are people striving to please the Lord in every way, no matter what. I believe that one of the major ways to "lift up Jesus" is through living a life of love, respect, goodness, and integrity.

Day 103

JESUS, DIVINE—THE SON OF THE LIVING GOD

Jesus existed in human form as the Jesus of history—broke into history to give His life as a ransom for mankind. He came to be an example of how we can also live for God in our humanity. He came because of His Supreme love for us all. He broke into history! He is also the Christ of faith, the Messiah, the Son of God. We believe that He is and the reward for those who diligently seek Him. By faith, we believe that He is God the Son! The God-Man!

Colossians 1:15-17
> *(15) He (Jesus Christ) is the image of the invisible God, the firstborn over all creation. (16) For by Him all things were created that are in heaven and that are on earth, visible and invisible, whether thrones or dominions or principalities or powers. All things were created through Him and for Him. (17) And He is before all things, and in Him all things consist. (NKJV)*

Colossians 2:9
> *For in Him (Christ) dwells all the fullness of the Deity (the Godhead) bodily. (NKJV)*

Christ lives in bodily form because He came all the way from heaven down to the earth to save a sinful generation. He lives! Colossians 1:15-17 and 2:9 are two of the strongest statements in the entire Bible about the divine nature of Jesus Christ. He is not only equal to God, but He *is* God. Jesus not only reflects God, He reveals God. He was the channel for God's glory, completely and totally. Being completely holy, He has the authority to judge the world. He said, "If you have seen me, you have also seen the Father." In Him is no clearer view of what God is like! Jesus is the one who we as humans can really relate to, because He has been in the likeness of sinful flesh Himself. He knows all about us. It is by Him that we can know God.

Now what did He do when He became a man? Jesus is the full revelation of God, the complete expression of God in a human body, Jesus is unique. He imposed on Himself all the time and space limitations that are imposed on all other human beings. Jesus had every opportunity to waste time, to get drunk, to be a glutton, to get angry, embittered, depressed, upset, frustrated, to have headaches, or to strike out at others. But in Him He displayed a Holy and Set apart life...He was and is an example of *true holiness*! Jesus was our example of how to live for God and to know Him. Through Jesus Christ, we can become true images of Christ—a portrait of Christ! He wants us to be like Him. He gave us a pattern and a model to follow.

Day 104

JESUS SAID "I AM THE WAY AND THE TRUTH AND THE LIFE"

John 14:6-10

(6) Jesus answered, "I am the way and the truth and the life. No one comes to the Father except through me. (7) If you really knew me, you would know my Father as well. From now on, you do know him and have seen him." (8) Philip said, "Lord, show us the Father and that will be enough for us." (9) Jesus answered: "Don't you know me, Philip, even after I have been among you such a long time? Anyone who has seen me has seen the Father. How can you say, 'Show us the Father'? (10) Don't you believe that I am in the Father, and that the Father is in me? The words I say to you are not just my own. Rather, it is the Father, living in me, who is doing his work.

Jesus is the way to salvation. Christ is the way to God. Through Jesus we can come to God. He is our mediator and our way of knowing more about God, the Father.

Jesus had to explain to His disciples who He was in relationship to knowing God. He told them that He was in the Father and the Father in Him—the Father is in me. Therefore, Jesus is our intercessor and our way to God! Jesus is saying, "If you want to see the mind and nature of God, if you want to see His attitudes, know more about the principles and character of God; look at Me (Jesus)." God reveals Himself and declares His glory to us through the life and works and words of Jesus Christ as He reveals Himself to our hearts and minds through the Holy Spirit (see John 14:6). Look to Jesus for all your needs.

Come to Jesus for total salvation and deliverance for the whole person. Jesus invites His followers to come to

Him for all of our needs. He promises to be the answer for them all, whether spiritually, emotionally, physically— in every way. That is a part of the plan for total and complete salvation and deliverance. It is just that simple!

Jesus is The Way because out of all of mankind, only He is unmarred by sin and has intimate knowledge of God. Knowing God depends on our knowledge of the truth about Jesus. He shows the way we must walk, the direction and manner of living and relating to others. This is precisely the knowledge Jesus gives. Many times we ask for directions in an unfamiliar city and the response confuses us because we are unfamiliar with the territory. But when we ask directions of Jesus, He says, "come, follow Me and I will take you there." You can never be lost with Jesus. Trust in His direction! Jesus is the way to complete salvation for the total man!

Day 105

LESSONS FROM THE BARREN FIG TREE ON FAITH IN JESUS CHRIST

Matthew 21:21-22
(21) The following verses are responses by Jesus Christ to questions from His disciples reference to The Barren Fig Tree. This is one of two teachings that Jesus gave using the fig tree as an object lesson. Jesus replied, "I tell you the truth, if you have faith and do not doubt, not only can you do what was done to the fig tree, but also you can say to this mountain 'Go, throw yourself into the sea,' and it will be done. (22) If you believe, you will receive whatever you ask for in prayer."

The scripture says that Jesus and the disciples were on their way back into the city early in the morning and He was hungry. He came upon a fig tree, but it was barren, except for leaves. Jesus condemned the fig tree and declared that it would not bear any fruit every again and the leaves withered. The disciples were amazed and wondered how that could happen so quickly. With this simple encounter with the fig tree, Jesus used this as an object lesson—a lesson of faith and trust. Jesus told them that if they would exercise faith and not doubt, they can do the same thing and even *greater* things. We must have faith in Jesus Christ when we pray for anything! This is so vital for success in our daily living! The deeper implication in this lesson is that a deep and abiding faith in Jesus will cause us not to worry about situations as one who does not believe in Jesus. Worry is the opposite of faith. Worry is counterproductive to our moving forward in life.

Worry comes about because we have lost control—we have no control of the situations that we face in life. Peace and tranquility come about when we turn our situations over to Jesus Christ completely! Many people, down through the years have gone through episodes of fear and distrust when facing difficult challenges of life. Those of us who trusted in Jesus have been successful in fighting and defeating the demons of fear and lack of faith.

Countless narratives of men and women throughout Bible history have left on record deeds, conflicts, problems, conquests, and also victories where faith in God brought them out. Jacob is one of them where he displayed fear and distress as he faced a difficult decision. The account is that he wrestled with an angel all night long and was determined that 'he would not let go until the

Lord blessed him.' Some scholars believe that he wrestled with God—fact is, he struggled and was blessed because of his strong faith in God. Faith gives us courage and strength—internal fortitude—the will to fight for our very lives. People of God, we *must* put our trust in God also for answers to our problems. Through God's Son Jesus Christ, it will be done (see Genesis 32:7)!

Day 106

LESSONS FROM THE PARABLE OF THE FIG TREE ON SIGNS OF THE END TIMES

Let's look at Luke 21:29-35 for Jesus' message from the Parable of the Fig Tree. This is the second message using the analogy of the fig tree as an object lesson:

(29) He told them this parable: "Look at the fig tree and all the trees. (30) When they sprout leaves, you can see for yourselves and know that summer is near. (31) Even so, when you see these things happening, you know that the kingdom of God is near. (32) "I tell you the truth this generation will certainly not pass away until all these things have happened. (33) Heaven and earth will pass away, but my words will never pass away. (34) "Be careful, or your hearts will be weighed down with dissipation, drunkenness and the anxieties of life, and that day will close on you unexpectedly like a trap. (35) For it will come upon all those who live on the face of the whole earth."

Christ relates the Parable of the Fig Tree (vv. 29-35) to give instruction regarding His warnings in the previous verses (vv. 8-28). Christ reminds His disciples to be watchful and not to be deceived when you hear of wars and rumors of wars; earthquakes, pestilences and famines in various places; great catastrophic events all over the land; and nations will be against nations. However, Jesus warns, do not be afraid or fearful, it is just signs of the times to come as the Kingdom end draws nigh. The end is near! Verses 12 and following address the suffering of ministry leaders and believers in general. There will be devastation and persecution in high and holy places. Christians everywhere will be devastated and persecuted. Jesus spoke of signs in the moon, sun, and the stars—anguish and perplexity—and to just be watchful and prayerful. The "these things" in verse 31 refers to the question asked in verse 7 concerning "When will 'these things' happen?" Therefore, Jesus gave the answer in the statements above in terms of the events foretold to happen as the end nears. In the parable, Christ provides the perspective we should have as we anticipate the unfolding of the previously described events—to be watchful and prayerful because we are aware of 'these things.'

What owner of a fig tree would spend hours each day scrutinizing his tree to see if it was budding? Would he make the fig tree the focal point of his day? Of course, no one would. An owner of a fig tree would be aware of its location, its level of health, and its progression through the annual cycle of growth, but these matters would not require his all-consuming effort. Don't spend all of your time worrying in fear about the things that are happening in the world today.

The parable, then, shows us that we should be aware of prophecy, we should keep an eye on what is happening in the world, but it does not require—and we should not allow it to become—our primary focus. Just know, the time of Jesus' return is drawing near. Be watchful, therefore, and be prayerful and stay in the race for our redemption draws nigh!

Day 107

THE PROBLEMS OF MANKIND, AND THE SOLUTIONS

Hebrews 10:32-36
(32) Remember those earlier days after you had received the light, when you stood your ground in a great contest (of life) in the face of suffering. (33) Sometimes you were publicly exposed to insult and persecution; at other times you stood side by side with those who were so treated. (34) You sympathized with those in prison and joyfully accepted the confiscation of your property, because you knew that you yourselves had better and lasting possessions. (35) So do not throw away your confidence; it will be richly rewarded. (36) You need to persevere so that when you have done the will of God, you will receive what he has promised.

With the problems of humanity being so great, many people resort to drugs and medicines that they believe will curtail their symptoms of anxiety and distress. Jesus is the answer for the total person. He is the way to life. Most of the top ten prescribed drugs in America are to treat worry and its associated symptoms. Despite our tendency to worry, the human body was not created to worry. It's like using a car that was meant to transport groceries to haul cement. When we are anxious, we compromise our health, and our body functions at a fraction of its capability. It has been said that "worrying is the interest we pay on a debt we might not owe." Worry costs us good health, mental and emotional stability, spiritual serenity and abundant life! Reduce your worrying today!

Jesus is the way the truth and the life! He is our deliverer! We must persevere with patience until we receive the promise from Jesus Christ! Worry and Fear are not the way Christ wants us to live. Fear and worry breeds an unhappy, defeatist life and may lead to the "walking dead." A walking death spiritually and emotionally and even physical death! As humans it is hard not to worry or fear. We all have this tendency, but I am encouraging all of us today to let Christ's 'Perfect Love cast out **all** fear!'

The Hebrews passage speaks to the Life of Faith practiced by the believer as being the answer for our present suffering—it is only temporary in that in due time 'in just a little while, Jesus is coming without delay. But in the mean time the righteous one will live by faith (verses 37-38). All we have to do is live for Jesus in faith and trust. Therefore, persevere with constancy, even under suffering if necessary with total trust in the Lord. Never surrender to the tactics of the enemy! Christ is our supreme deliverer and restorer!

Day 108

GIVING OF YOUR TOTAL SELF

It should be noted that God wants us to give our time, talent, and treasure—our entire being to His service. Giving is a blessing to the individual; to the Body of Christ; to the world, and the Kingdom of God. It is a blessing to give! Not giving is a curse! Fact is, God said, 'it is more blessed to give than to receive.'

Malachi 3:8-10

> *(8) "Will a man rob God? Yet you rob me. "But you ask, 'How do we rob you?' In tithes and offerings." (9) You are under a curse—the whole nation of you—because you are robbing me. (10) Bring the whole tithe into the storehouse, that there may be food in my house. Test me in this," says the LORD Almighty, "and see if I will not throw open the floodgates of heaven and pour out so much blessing that you will not have room enough for it.*

The people of Malachi's day had let God down; their attitude was terrible after all God had done for them, and the thing is they didn't even realize it. They presented God with just anything; it was not sufficient as a gift or sacrifice for the Lord Almighty. Therefore, they were guilty of robbing God, not only in their giving, but in their total life. That is an important point to note in that whenever a person fails to offer gifts to the Lord, it also affects the offering of oneself to the service of the Lord. The Lord wants our total commitment to His service.

Even though we belong to God, we let Him down in many ways. Some realize it by simply being selfish and others miss it unaware. A person can let God down in the way we disregard His doctrine causing a lack of faith individually and in the brotherhood. People of God can also let God down in our offerings—the offering of our lives. We can let God down in our marriages by not loving our spouses, or we can let Him down in not correctly raising our children. God wants a pure heart within us, and He wants us to obey Him in every facet of our lives, not just in tithing, but including all our skills. We can let God down in study and prayer. We can let God down in not putting God first. This is short-changing God. Don't short-change God! Give Him your all today! This is as aspect of stewardship. A part of loving is giving and giving loving.

Consider what God did for you. He gave His Son, the greatest gift and offering of all gifts. That was the ultimate best that God could possibly give—all because He loves us! Jesus Christ gave Himself freely—not under constraint, but willingly, for us and for everyone in this world! What should we be giving back? We should be doing our very best to overcome and thus not rob God by not giving of ourselves completely and not being a living sacrifice. Because of the people (Israel) letting God down so much, God says, "You are cursed with a curse - even this whole nation!" You don't want to be cursed with a curse! No way! You don't want to be a part of the problem, but the solution. What we do can affect the entire nation (community) and the church and it robs God. What you give or don't give can affect others. Obedience to God is better than sacrifice!

Day 109

THE MINISTRY OF THE GOD-MAN

Luke 4:14-19
(14) And Jesus returned in the power of the Spirit into Galilee, and news of Him went out through all the surrounding region. (15) And He taught in their synagogues, being glorified by all. (16) So He came to Nazareth, where He had been brought up. And as His custom was, He went into the synagogue on the Sabbath day, and stood up to read. (17) And He was handed

the book of the prophet Isaiah. And when He had opened the book, He found the place where it was written: (18) "The Spirit of the Lord is upon Me, because He has anointed Me to preach the gospel to the poor; He has sent Me to heal the broken-hearted, to proclaim liberty to the captives and recovery of sight to the blind, to set at liberty those who are oppressed; (19) To proclaim the acceptable year of the Lord." (NKJV)

The passage contains the activity of Jesus' divine attributes and human virtues. In the above verses and on through verse 30 Jesus proclaims the Year of Jubilee—the jubilee of grace—and gives a statement of His ministry (His commission) as Savior, as God's Anointed One, as the Messiah to His people. He gives His mandate to proclaim the gospel to those who are poor—in heavenly, spiritual divine things. He came to release the captives: the persecuted, the exiled, and those who are under Satan's bondage (see also Isa 42:7). You don't have to be bound! Jesus has set you free!

The ministry of the God-man is also for us today. He uses His disciples to perform His mission. The ministry of Jesus also is to bring recovery of sight to the blind physically and spiritually—that is, to release from bondage under the power of Satan and his forces. Releasing those who are persecuted and oppressed by Satan, and then to proclaiming the year of jubilee! Proclaiming victory in Jesus Christ!

Day 110

THE BENEDICTION

Ephesians 3:20-21
   *(20) Now to Him who is able to do exceedingly abundantly
   above all that we ask or think, according to the power that works
   in us, (21) To Him be glory in the church by Christ Jesus to all
   generations, forever and ever. Amen. (NKJV)*

Those final verses in Ephesians are a powerful
benediction affirming Christ's power to all generations.
They acknowledge His power to go beyond what we can
ask or think. It is difficult to comprehend the
immeasurable power of Jesus Christ to perform what we
need Him to.

In the earlier verses, the apostle Paul prays to the
Father in verse 14 that the saints may be strengthened in
the inner man and the Father answers through the Spirit in
verse 16 that Christ the Son of God (in verse 17) may
make His abode in our hearts through all generations.
Jesus will be forever present in our hearts and minds! We
are, therefore, filled with the fullness of God—the Triune
God! The Father, The Son, and The Holy Spirit! He will
flood our very being with His Spirit forever and ever.
Christ will do exceedingly abundantly above *all* we may ask
or think. Amen.

ABOUT THE AUTHOR

Rev. Hugh Anderson, II is the founder of Solid Rock Ministry Network Church of God in Christ (COGIC) presently in Winter Park/Orlando, FL. He began pastoral ministry as assistant pastor at Anderson Memorial COGIC in High Springs, FL and Westside COGIC in Alachua, FL under the pastorate of the late Supt. Hugh Anderson, Sr. He is an ordained Elder in the Church of God in Christ, Inc. and has pastored Pine Street COGIC in Starke, FL; Solid Rock Evangelistic Center COGIC in Gainesville, FL; and Latter Rain Harvest Ministries COGIC in Gainesville, FL.

Rev. Anderson was a band and choral director at Interlachen High School in Putnam County, FL and a Substance Abuse Counselor at two State of Florida Prisons. His speaking engagements have included international conferences, rallies, interdenominational worship services, and revival/crusade speaker at several venues.

He was honorably discharged from the United States Army in 1969 as a Military Intelligence Analyst during the Vietnam War Era.

He holds a Bachelor of Science in Music Education with a concentration in piano and voice from the Florida Agricultural and Mechanical University in Tallahassee, FL. Rev. Anderson also received the Master of Divinity degree from C.H. Mason Theological Seminary (a constituent of the Interdenominational Theological Center) in Atlanta, GA in 1980. His Master's concentrations were Psychology of Pastoral Care and Counseling and Biblical Studies: Old and New Testament. Here he excelled in Homiletics, receiving the Isaac R. Clarke preaching award.

Rev. Anderson was married to the late Fernsene L. Anderson and is the father of five children.